PRINCE FAGGOT

Also by Jordan Tannahill

Age of Minority: Three Solo Plays
Botticelli in the Fire & Sunday in Sodom
Concord Floral
Is My Microphone On?
Late Company

PRINCE

Jordan Tannahill

FAGGOT

PLAYWRIGHTS CANADA PRESS

TORONTO

Prince Faggot © 2025 by Jordan Tannahill
First edition: November 2025. Second printing: December 2025.
Printed and bound in Canada by Imprimerie Gauvin Ltée, Gatineau

Jacket art and design by Tom Etherington
Author photo by Sam Waxman

Playwrights Canada Press
202-269 Richmond St. W., Toronto, ON M5V 1X1
416.703.0013 | info@playwrightscanada.com | www.playwrightscanada.com

For professional or amateur production rights, please contact:
Colin Rivers, Marquis Literary
www.mqlit.ca | colin@mqent.ca

LIBRARY AND ARCHIVES CANADA CATALOGUING IN PUBLICATION
Title: Prince Faggot / Jordan Tannahill.
Names: Tannahill, Jordan, author.
Identifiers: Canadiana (print) 20250267535 | Canadiana (ebook) 20250274698
  | ISBN 9780369105943 (softcover) | ISBN 9780369105967 (EPUB)
  | ISBN 9780369105950 (PDF)
Subjects: LCGFT: Drama.
Classification: LCC PS8639.A577 P75 2025 | DDC C812/.6—dc23

Playwrights Canada Press staff work across Turtle Island, on Treaty 13 and Treaty 20 territories, as well as unceded lands, which are the current, ancestral, and future homes of the Anishinaabe Nations (Ojibwe / Chippewa, Odawa, Potawatomi, Algonquin, Saulteaux, Nipissing, and Mississauga / Michi Saagiig), the Wendat, members of the Haudenosaunee Confederacy (Mohawk, Oneida, Onondaga, Cayuga, Seneca, and Tuscarora), and the xʷməθkʷəy̓əm (Musqueam), Sḵwx̱wú7mesh (Squamish), and səlilwətaɬ (Tsleil-Waututh) Nations, as well as Metis and Inuit peoples. It always was and always will be Indigenous land.

We acknowledge the financial support of the Canada Council for the Arts, the Ontario Arts Council (OAC), Ontario Creates, the Government of Ontario, and the Government of Canada for our publishing activities.

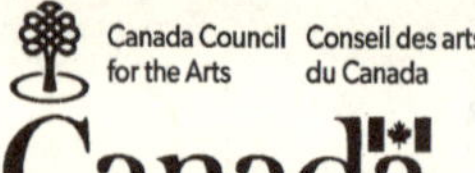  

For Brandon

Prince Faggot was first produced by Playwrights Horizons and Soho Rep by special arrangement with Jeremy O. Harris and Josh Godfrey of bb² at the Peter Jay Sharp Theater, New York City, from May 30 to August 3, 2025, with the following cast and creative team:

Performers: Rachel Crowl, K. Todd Freeman, David Greenspan, Mihir Kumar, John McCrea, and N'yomi Allure Stewart

Director: Shayok Misha Chowdhury
Scenic Designer: David Zinn
Costume Designer: Montana Levi Blanco
Lighting Designer: Isabella Byrd
Sound Designer and Original Music: Lee Kinney
Wig and Hair Designer: Cookie Jordan
Associate Director: Jack Serio
Dramaturg: Sarah Lunnie
Intimacy Coordination: UnkleDave's Fight-House
Production Stage Manager: Ryan Gohsman

Note on Text

Performer 4's final monologue was inspired by a rehearsal hall interview with actress N'yomi Allure Stewart. All other text in the show, including the direct address monologues, is fictional and written by the playwright.

A backslash (/) connotes when the next line begins, in overlap.

A pause is longer than a beat, which is no more than a breath.

Cast

Performer 1
Dev Chatterjee

Performer 2
William, Prince of Wales
Richard the Lionheart

Performer 3
Catherine (Kate), Princess of Wales
Queen Anne
Correspondent 1

Performer 4
Charlotte, Princess of Wales
King James I
Astrid, a servant
Paramedic

Performer 5
Jaqueline Davies, communications director
Andrew Farmer, a butler
King Edward II
Correspondent 2

Performer 6
Prince George

1.

An ensemble of six performers appear in their street clothes.

They begin changing into costumes kept on racks visible on either side of the stage.

PERFORMER 1 steps forward.

PERFORMER 1
This is a photograph of me at the age of four.

A real photograph of PERFORMER 1 at the age of four is projected.

In their own words, the performer takes a moment to describe the photograph. Where it was taken, who took the image, what the performer is doing in the photograph, etc.

I found this photo as I was helping my mum move out of her apartment. It fell out of an old album, and the moment I picked it up I just burst out laughing because it was so overwhelmingly obvious: even at the age of four I was a fairy. I can't even tell you exactly what combination of signifiers in this image prompted this realization, but for me it was like, immediate. Like—wow, okay. And it set off this little chain reaction of memories of crushes I had on boyhood friends, and the older brothers of friends, when I was like five and six, which I had completely pushed from my mind.

This photo felt like some kind of proof that, as a four-year-old, I was not a queer man in waiting. I was a queer child. I was queer in the present tense. And obviously at four I still had no conception of what sex was, but I had a sexuality—an ever-evolving relationship to my body and my gender, and the bodies and genders of others. For me this photo felt like proof that I was actually an unbroken continuum of being. And as I held this photo I was reminded of another image of a four-year-old boy that had prompted that exact same laugh of recognition in me.

> A *photograph of Prince* GEORGE *of Wales, at the age of four, is projected.*

Prince George of Wales in 2017, gazing with limpid amazement at an ascending helicopter. Now, I am far from the first queen to clock George in this photo. I remember literally hundreds of people on social media sharing this photo and calling George a "gay icon" for his adorably fey pose. There were articles and think pieces about it. And I shared one of these posts on Twitter, you know, as one did. And I got pulled into this vicious thread with an old school friend about it, and she was like, you know—

PERFORMER 5
This is really outrageous and sick.

PERFORMER 1
And I was like—okay, let's talk about that.

PERFORMER 5
I have a five-year-old son.

PERFORMER 1
Yup, we've all seen the photos.

PERFORMER 5
Can you imagine someone writing that about him?

PERFORMER 1 *looks at the audience.*

Sexualizing a young child like that is disgusting.

PERFORMER 1
Walk away, right, that's when you just—put your phone down. But I'm not so good at that. And, in fairness, she was challenging me to think critically about this. So I was like, okay, Kendra—her name's Kendra—can you not see how all children are "sexualized" as heterosexual by default? Heterosexuality is projected onto children from literally the moment they're born. To make my point, I posted this *Cosmopolitan* article from 2014 about how the eight-month-old Prince George—

The Cosmopolitan *article is projected.*

PERFORMER 3
—managed to draw all attention away from his mother and her hair by receiving a marriage proposal from an older woman—an eleven-month-old cougar by the name of Ruby Cate Blitz popped out of the crowd wearing a T-shirt bearing the message, "Marry Me George."

PERFORMER 1
And I was like, do you have a problem with this article, Kendra? And obviously she did because she blocked me. But that exchange really got me thinking about this. Children are never too young to be sexualized in the heterosexual consciousness. My papa, my grandfather, used to ask me when I was three and four if I had a girlfriend yet.

One of the other photographs of Prince GEORGE, *staring up
at the helicopter at the age of four, is projected.*

Look, the queers in the audience—and I'm assuming that's most
of you, let's be honest—we know one of our own when we see one
because we ourselves were once queer children. We can locate our
younger selves in photos of George's poses and prancing because
the world taught us to notice and isolate and suppress these
affects—or suffer the consequences. And listen, I know there's no
easy correlative between behaviour and sexuality. Effeminate traits
are beaten out of hetero men just as much as they're beaten out of
us. But. As long as the Kendras of the world continue to impose a
heterosexual default on all children, it is an act of compassion to
give shelter to this effete little prince under the broad umbrella of
queerness.

PERFORMER 2
Ooo weee.

PERFORMER 2 *points to an unspecified person in the
audience.*

This poor woman over here with her arms crossed is thinking what-
in-the-name-of-Pizzagate have I gotten myself into?

PERFORMER 1
Obviously I can't predict the full, luscious scope of George's
sexuality and gender—

PERFORMER 2
No you cannot.

PERFORMER 1
But as I look at this photo of this little royal fawn, in his purple
checked shirt and navy shorts, clasping his face like a model

in a perfume ad, I can't help but feel this immense sense of
protectiveness toward him, and—

PERFORMER 2
And does your protectiveness extend to showing this photograph to
a theatre of a hundred and twenty-eight strangers?

PERFORMER 1
This photo is on the Internet, it was published in thousands of
newspapers—

PERFORMER 2
(*to audience*) My position—I understand where [Performer 1] is
coming from here, but to me, that's still projecting onto a child.
Like, I get that queerness isn't some switch suddenly flipped one
day at the age of thirteen, but there is a real child here—

PERFORMER 1
I know that, / and that real child—

PERFORMER 2
Things have gotten so hot in this country— You start talking about
queer childhood, they're gonna brand you a groomer, okay, they'll
fucking dox you. We've got neo-Nazis with semi-automatic rifles
shutting down drag queen story hours out there.

PERFORMER 1
That's exactly my point, we can't even have a nuanced
conversation about these things—

PERFORMER 2
And I'm saying leave this real child out of all that shit.

PERFORMER 5
Frankly, I think we've been doing a terrible job with the grooming.
I mean look how many straights there are still.

PERFORMER 1
(*to* PERFORMER 2) Let's see the photograph of you at the age of
five, then.

A *childhood photograph of* PERFORMER 2 *is projected.*

PERFORMER 2
This is actually me at the age of ten or eleven. Very butch as you can
see. And look, I know I wasn't exactly the straightest of children.

PERFORMER 3
Honey, no one was saying that.

PERFORMER 2
No one was saying that about you either, girl.

A *childhood photograph of* PERFORMER 3 *is projected.*

PERFORMER 3
I know they weren't! (*considers herself/himself/themselves in the
photo*) I mean just look at that gorgeous little bird.

PERFORMER 1
(*to* PERFORMER 2, *pointing to the photo*) Are you going to tell me the
hetero default served this child?

PERFORMER 3
No! It fucked me up for years.

PERFORMER 2
So would projecting her photograph in an off-Broadway theatre.

PERFORMER 3
(*points to herself/himself/themselves in the photo*) Oh I don't know, girl, not that child—she would've loved this.

> PERFORMER 1 *turns to* PERFORMER 5.

PERFORMER 1
You were a queer child, [Performer 5].

> A *photo of* PERFORMER 5 *as a child is projected.*

PERFORMER 5
Oh yes, there he is.

PERFORMER 1
[Performer 6], you were a queer child.

> A *photo of* PERFORMER 6 *as a child is projected.*

PERFORMER 3
(*to* PERFORMER 6) What was that, about five years ago?

PERFORMER 1
And [Performer 4]—

PERFORMER 4
The thing is when I was a kid my mom was always telling me to throw up duces or not smile too much or, you know, "Why you always cocking your head to the side?" because she knew, right. She was always trying to get me to pose like a little boy should. So I wonder what my queer childhood photo would've really looked like, you know what I mean? If I'd been allowed to have one.

PERFORMER 2
My point remains. We're talking about a real child.

PERFORMER 1
And look, I get that. And I also get that, you know, as much as we might recognize our younger selves in Prince George, I also recognize we are *not* the same, and never will be. Right? I'm a broke Brown actor who lives in a rented apartment that I share with two other grown adults. Prince George will never once, in his life, not even for a single second, consider my existence. I will, on the other hand, see his face on screens and newspapers every week, multiple times a week, until the day I die. And that is what got us thinking—if Prince George *were* to be an openly gay king, and the first royal to have a gay wedding—what does that mean for us queers? Will we recognize ourselves in that? Is he supposed to embody our aspirations? Where does that leave us in the story? And who gets to tell that story?

PERFORMER 4
Well, tonight we do.

PERFORMER 2
An act of queer prognostication.

PERFORMER 5
Tonight—

PERFORMER 3
We imagine that story for you.

PERFORMER 2
A psychic reclamation.

PERFORMER 1
Tonight the queers are royals, and the royals are the subject.

PERFORMER 4
Tonight the subject is faggotry.

PERFORMER 2
Yes, to be clear, we are still very much the subject of this show.

PERFORMER 1
(*to* PERFORMER 2) Yes there's a real child named George, but obviously this is not his story, only he can write that for himself. This is our story.

PERFORMER 3
And this is our George.

PERFORMER 5
A fabulation.

PERFORMER 4
Queer spirits and magic.

PERFORMER 1
We're in a theatre after all.

PERFORMER 2
The faggot's palace.

PERFORMER 1
So allow me to set the stage for you all. This, as I'm sure you know, is [Performer 2].

PERFORMER 2
And tonight I will be playing the role of William, Prince of Wales.

PERFORMER 3
My name is [Performer 3], and I will be playing his wife, Catherine.

PERFORMER 4
My name is [Performer 4], and I will be giving you full House of Windsor glamour as their daughter, Princess Charlotte.

PERFORMER 1

This over here is the ravishing [Performer 5].

PERFORMER 5

I will be playing the royal butler, Andrew Farmer. And also the royal communications director, Jaqueline Davies.

PERFORMER 1

My name is [Performer 1], and I will be playing the role of Dev Chatterjee.

PERFORMER 2

And finally, this here is [Performer 6], and [they/she/he] will, of course, be playing the role of—

Lights shift.

2.

KATE
George. Enough.

A room in Kensington Palace.

GEORGE, *eighteen, and his parents,* KATE *and* WILLIAM, *are in the midst of an argument while doing other things.*

GEORGE
Lottie's bringing Sarah!

WILLIAM
Sarah's family — it's a family weekend.

KATE
We haven't even met this Dev.

GEORGE
Because you haven't wanted to.

KATE
That's not true.

GEORGE
Well now's your chance.

WILLIAM
The matter's closed.

KATE
If you want to have a friends' weekend at Anmer before summer starts—

GEORGE
He's not just a friend.

    Pause.

/ You know that.

KATE
Oh. I—

GEORGE
We're seeing each other. Obviously.

KATE
Dev?

GEORGE
Obviously, yes.

KATE
Well it wasn't— *(to WILLIAM)* Was it obvious to you?

WILLIAM
No.

KATE
I had no idea—your father and I both didn't realize Dev was your partner.

GEORGE
He's my boyfriend, he's not my partner.

KATE
Well, whatever, we—

GEORGE
It's not whatever for me.

KATE
No, I know, I'm not— We're obviously very happy for you, Tips.
You know that.

GEORGE
Well.

GEORGE *gestures.*

WILLIAM
Thank you for telling us.

GEORGE
You already knew.

KATE
We didn't.

WILLIAM
It doesn't matter.

KATE
No. It doesn't. We love you with all of our heart, and we're thrilled
that you're—you know, that you're seeing someone who makes you
happy.

GEORGE
Except you don't want to meet him.

KATE
Oh come on, of course we do.

GEORGE
So can he come to Anmer?

    KATE *looks at* WILLIAM.

KATE
Yes, of course. That would be lovely.

GEORGE
Okay. Thank you.

WILLIAM
What's his last name?

GEORGE
You don't know his family.

WILLIAM
I just want to know his name.

GEORGE
Chatterjee.

WILLIAM
Pardon?

GEORGE
Dev Chatterjee.

WILLIAM
Oh interesting.

KATE
What's he studying?

GEORGE
Same as me. History of art.

WILLIAM
Can I ask, does anyone at Oxford —?

GEORGE
Just close friends, very close.

WILLIAM
How many?

GEORGE
Just five or six.

WILLIAM
Well then everyone knows.

GEORGE
No, they don't.

WILLIAM
Five or six —?

GEORGE
We've been very cautious.

WILLIAM
How long has it been?

GEORGE
A couple of months. But we've been friends for a while.

WILLIAM
And the two of you, when you're out and about—?

GEORGE
No, we don't hold hands, Daddy, we don't kiss. I told Dev we couldn't do any of that until I'd spoken to both of you and to Jaqueline.

WILLIAM
Right, well, she'll definitely want to know about this as soon as possible. In fact, speaking of Jaqueline—

KATE
No, not speaking of Jaqueline, I want to hear more about Dev. Tell us what he's like.

GEORGE
Well. He's very smart. Um. He's a little bit older than me. He's a grad student.

KATE
Okay.

WILLIAM
Four years older?

GEORGE
Yeah. Four years older. He's very cultured, very worldly, you'll, you'll see next weekend, I guess.

KATE
Well I can't wait to meet him.

WILLIAM
Me too. We're very happy for you, Tips.

KATE
Come here.

GEORGE *walks over to* KATE, *and she embraces him, gives him a kiss.*

WILLIAM *does the same.*

Why are you crying?

GEORGE
I'm not, I don't know, you're crying too.

KATE
Only because you are.

They laugh.

WILLIAM
You're going to make me start.

KATE
You weren't worried about telling us, were you?

GEORGE
A little, maybe.

WILLIAM
We're behind you one hundred percent, and we'll make sure this is framed the right way. We've got to be prepared for the fact that there'll be idiots out there, maybe even some press, who'll want to tear you both down, and who'll probably say some / really nasty things.

KATE
The press won't.

WILLIAM
Well, if we get this right. But I think the overwhelming response is going to be very positive, very supportive —

KATE
Very supportive.

GEORGE
I hope so.

KATE
Absolutely.

GEORGE
The one thing. It's kind of dumb but. I don't want to tell Grandpa.

KATE
Why?

GEORGE
I mean myself. You can tell him.

KATE
Everyone's going to be very supportive.

GEORGE
I know, I just don't really want to have that conversation with him, that's all.

There is a knock at the door. Andrew FARMER *enters.*

FARMER
Sorry to interrupt, Your Royal Highness. Your three o'clock is waiting in the drawing room.

WILLIAM
Thank you, Farmer, tell him I'll be right there.

FARMER *nods and exits.*

KATE
Do Charlotte and Louis know?

GEORGE
Charlotte does.

WILLIAM
Anyone else in the palace?

GEORGE
Just Farmer.

KATE *gestures toward the door.*

KATE
You told the butler?

GEORGE
He's the first person I came out to, actually.

WILLIAM
When?

GEORGE
Um. I'd say about five years ago.

Lights shift.

The performers begin changing into new costumes.

PERFORMER 4
Girl, the look in Kate's eyes like—wait, my little baby came out to
our gay butler?

PERFORMER 3
Alarm bells!

PERFORMER 4
Groomer!

PERFORMER 5
He's George's confidant.

PERFORMER 3
But coming out to the staff?

PERFORMER 5
Andrew Farmer has known the kids their entire lives.

PERFORMER 6
A weekend at Anmer Hall. William and Kate's ten-bedroom
Georgian country house in Norfolk, about three kilometres down
the road from Sandringham. The year is 2032. Charles is still king.
For the first time a hurricane has been stopped by human interven-
tion, and a 3D-printed liver has been successfully transplanted. As
the car carrying Dev and George turns off the country road onto
the long approach to Anmer Hall, and Dev sees the manor house
in the distance, he thinks to himself—

DEV
My god, I'm in a fucking Keira Knightley movie. Remember this
moment, remember the light, remember the feeling of his hand in
your hand on the leather of this back seat.

　　Lights shift.

3.

Anmer Hall.

As DEV *and* GEORGE *arrive, they are greeted by* KATE *and* WILLIAM.

WILLIAM
There they are! How was the journey?

GEORGE
Fine, thanks. Uneventful.

WILLIAM
Dev. So nice to meet you.

DEV *bows his head, as is protocol.*

DEV
It's an honour, Your Royal Highness.

WILLIAM *extends his hand to shake* DEV's.

WILLIAM
Please, call me William.

KATE
And I'm Kate. Lovely to meet you.

DEV *bows his head while shaking* KATE's *hand.*

DEV
Thank you so much for having me. This is really . . .

DEV *gestures.*

KATE
George has spoken very highly of you.

DEV
Well. That's very nice of him. I'm sure some of it's true.

WILLIAM
Did you see the sky?

GEORGE
Yes, beautiful.

DEV
I uh—I got you both a little something as a token of my appreciation.

KATE
Oh how lovely. You really didn't have to.

DEV *hands* KATE *a box.*

Let's move into the drawing room, shall we, and open it there. Would you like something to drink, Dev? Some tea, some wine— red, white?

They begin moving into the drawing room.

DEV
A glass of red would be lovely, thank you.

KATE turns to ASTRID, *the servant, and nods.* ASTRID *exits.*

WILLIAM
So—

KATE proffers the gift to WILLIAM.

KATE
Did you want to do the honours?

WILLIAM
No, no.

KATE
It's beautifully wrapped.

KATE unwraps the box and takes out a book.

Oh how lovely. Virginia Woolf's *The Waves*.

DEV
It's the original edition actually, from 1931.

WILLIAM
Is it?

KATE
How remarkable.

DEV
Have you read it?

KATE
You know, I haven't.

KATE turns to WILLIAM.

Have you?

WILLIAM
No.

KATE
I had to read *Mrs. Dalloway* for school, I remember liking it very much. You know, it's been ages since I've read a book. He's reading that new Churchill biography at the moment.

WILLIAM
Apparently, yes. I mostly just carry it around with me.

KATE
Well, thank you so much, that's incredibly thoughtful of you.

GEORGE
Are Lottie and Sarah here?

KATE
They're in the garden

GEORGE
We should go say hi.

WILLIAM
Just, just before you do—I didn't want to spring this on you both right away, but—

WILLIAM *turns to* DEV.

Our lovely communications secretary, Jaqueline, has insisted that the five of us sit down for a little emergency meeting.

GEORGE
Emergency?

KATE
There's no emergency.

WILLIAM
There's been some press interest in you, Dev.

GEORGE
What? How? Already?

WILLIAM
We just all need to be on the same page. And this is really the first and only chance we're going to have to sit down and go over everything.

GEORGE
You mean this weekend?

WILLIAM
I suggested a video call, but she insisted on meeting Dev in person.

GEORGE
Wait, what, she's coming here?

WILLIAM
She should be arriving in the next few minutes.

GEORGE
Why? That's crazy. We've just arrived.

DEV
I really don't mind.

WILLIAM
She's working to very tight deadlines.

GEORGE
Why didn't you give us any notice? This, this feels like an ambush.

WILLIAM
There's a situation that's come up. I'm not going / to get into it now.

GEORGE
What situation?

WILLIAM
I'm not getting into it now, we'll wait for Jaqueline.

KATE
Sorry about this, Dev, this is not usually how we greet our guests.

DEV
That's quite all right.

ASTRID *reappears.*

ASTRID
Sorry to interrupt, Your Royal Highness, but / Ms. Davies is here.

JAQUELINE *strides into the front hall.*

JAQUELINE
That sunset! My god. What are you all doing cooped up in here, you're missing the big show.

WILLIAM
We're waiting for you is what we're doing.

JAQUELINE
Hi, everyone, hello, hello. You must be Dev. I'm Jaqueline.

DEV
Nice to meet you.

JAQUELINE
Enchanté.

KATE
They literally just walked in the door.

JAQUELINE
Ah, perfect timing then. *(to DEV)* Look at you. You are so much more handsome than in photographs.

KATE
Would you like something to drink?

JAQUELINE
Yes, a San Pellegrino, thank you.

ASTRID *exits.*

All right. I know you want to get on with your evening, so let's get down to business here. Dev. Sweetheart. I wanted to meet you in person because we'll be working closely together for some time to come *(glances at GEORGE)* hopefully. And tomorrow morning is going to be a very, very big day for you, because that's the day the world is going to discover who Dev Chatterjee is. You will be trending. Your photo will be in every tabloid in this country. And I'm here to help you navigate that, okay?

DEV
And sorry, why exactly—?

JAQUELINE
(to WILLIAM*)* Oh did you not tell them yet? *(to* DEV *and* GEORGE*)*
Well, boys, there's a photograph of the two of you holding hands at
the Oxford train station on your way up here from earlier today.

GEORGE
What?

DEV
Holding hands?

GEORGE
Can I see?

> JAQUELINE *pulls her phone out of her purse and brings up*
> *the photograph.*

JAQUELINE
Some poor sod posted it on X instead of selling it to *The Mirror*.
Could've paid his rent for months.

> JAQUELINE *hands the phone to* GEORGE.

GEORGE
I don't even—I mean this would've been for a split second.

> GEORGE *hands the phone to* DEV.

JAQUELINE
It's very sweet, but naturally the royal correspondents have been
hounding me all day, and I need to know the official line to take
with them.

GEORGE
Well I—I'm not going to make some big announcement.

JAQUELINE
Of course not.

WILLIAM
No one's asking for that.

DEV *hands the phone back to* JAQUELINE.

JAQUELINE
But it also doesn't serve you to hide at this point. We can control the story, or they can. The thing is, Dev—I just learned about you two days ago, so I'm playing catch-up here. So, first thing's first, can I publicly confirm that the two of you are dating?

GEORGE
Yes, that's fine. *(turns to* DEV*)* Right?

DEV
Of course.

JAQUELINE
For how long?

GEORGE
Almost three months.

JAQUELINE
Really? Well they're going to want to feel a lot closer to the action than that. Let's say three weeks. How'd you meet?

GEORGE *and* DEV *share a look.*

GEORGE
Um—

JAQUELINE
Let's say through a mutual friend.

GEORGE
Jaqueline, you know I love you, but you really didn't have to come all this way to ask us this.

JAQUELINE
(to DEV) I came here to look you in the eyes and tell you that your life is going to change and we need to prepare you for that, because right now, sweetheart, you are not prepared. I've done my homework on you, and I have to be honest, I was quite concerned with what I found. You've had a very active online presence for some time now. Your X and Instagram are very political—

WILLIAM
Political in what way exactly?

DEV
Well. I've—I mean I've had them for many years, so I've made posts about a range of topics.

WILLIAM
Like—?

DEV
Um—

JAQUELINE
I made a list, actually. *(reading from her phone)* Demilitarization of the police, transgender bathroom access, universal basic income, funding of the NHS, arms deals to Saudi Arabia, / state surveillance—

WILLIAM
I-I don't need a full list, that's fine.

JAQUELINE
It's significant.

DEV
It is.

JAQUELINE
I also found six articles you wrote for *The Oxford Student* on various topics in the visual arts.

DEV
Yes.

JAQUELINE
Including a think piece you wrote on the pederastic gaze in Attic pottery-painting.

KATE
The pederastic gays?

JAQUELINE
G-a-z-e.

KATE
I see.

GEORGE
They're very good articles.

DEV
Surely those aren't an issue?

JAQUELINE
Anything can be made an issue. The way you close a car door can be an issue. They are going to find every single scrap they can on you, and we have to be ready with a response when they do.

DEV
Okay.

JAQUELINE
As we speak your social media's being mined for content.

DEV
But only my X account is public, the rest—

JAQUELINE
Sweetheart, you let Beth Andrews follow you five hours ago on Instagram, who do you think that was? *(points to herself)* They will find their way in; they'll pay your friends if they need to.

DEV
I-I'll just delete them all now.

    DEV *gets out his phone and begins deleting his social media accounts.*

GEORGE
Well this is all very stressful.

JAQUELINE
It didn't have to be. You could've given me a little bit more notice, love.

WILLIAM
I'm sorry, that's partially my fault—I promised George I would speak to you.

JAQUELINE
He's a big boy, he could've done it himself. Listen, I'm not here to spook you, but I'm not going to sugar-coat it either.

ASTRID *returns with the two glasses of red wine and*
JAQUELINE*'s San Pellegrino.*

DEV
Thank you.

JAQUELINE
Thank you, Astrid.

KATE
Are you hungry? Dev?

DEV
Oh I'm fine, thank you.

JAQUELINE
I am a bit, actually.

KATE
Could we get a few snacks?

JAQUELINE
No meat. Thank you.

ASTRID *nods and exits.*

Something I wanted to flag, sweetheart, in your review of the Kara Walker exhibition at the Tate Modern last March. You wrote—let me see if I have it here—you wrote about the show's anti-imperialist themes and the "lingering stain of slavery" on the British monarchy.

DEV
I did. Yes.

WILLIAM
They're definitely going to run with that.

JAQUELINE
Well, quite.

GEORGE
I've read that review and it makes absolute sense in the context of the—of-of the artist's work. It's not a personal opinion Dev is expressing.

JAQUELINE
Yes, but I rather doubt *The Mail* will be teasing out those nuances.

WILLIAM
Sorry, do you mind if I see the article?

JAQUELINE
Yes I— I think I have it on a tab, yes, here you go.

    JAQUELINE *pulls up the article on her phone and hands it to* WILLIAM.

DEV
To be clear, it does feature my personal opinions—it's a review after all.

GEORGE
Right, but—

DEV
But the facts are that Walker's work, in that show—I mean it explic-
itly dealt with the British imperial slave trade.

JAQUELINE
And no one is criticizing or questioning the content, it's just something we have to be aware of coming down the line.

KATE
Who's this artist, sorry?

JAQUELINE
We have to anticipate some people calling you a hypocrite, or
think pieces / in *The Guardian* about some—

DEV
Because I—? I'm sorry, but just because / I wrote a review—

JAQUELINE
I'm not saying that I think you are, but papers may write that.

WILLIAM
It's very well written.

    WILLIAM *hands the phone back to* JAQUELINE.

DEV
Thank you.

    JAQUELINE *turns to* DEV.

JAQUELINE
I need to know the skeletons in your closet. Family dynamics,
people with axes to grind, that sort of thing. I don't want to be

caught off-guard. And I'm not going to make you spill the beans right now in front of your new in-laws—not in-laws but you know what I mean—but I'll be following up with you about all that in the next day or so, yeah?

DEV
When it comes to my family, you really don't have to worry.

JAQUELINE
Well, you say that now, but they will find things, trust me.

DEV
I really doubt it.

JAQUELINE
Your mother was born in Chandigarh; your father grew up in Leeds; they got married, moved to Barking, and separated when you were four. You grew up with your father, who ran a computer store for eleven years before filing for bankruptcy and now collects disability for his MS.

DEV
You could work for MI5.

GEORGE
Oh MI5 has nothing on Jaqueline.

JAQUELINE
First student from your school ever to get into Oxbridge.

DEV
I uh—I hate to be rude, but can I excuse myself to use the toilet?

KATE
Oh of course, after that long trip, and we've just pounced on you the moment you walked in. George, can you show him where it is?

GEORGE
Yeah, just this way.

> JAQUELINE, KATE, *and* WILLIAM *continue a conversation, unheard, as* DEV *and* GEORGE *walk out of the room into the hallway.*

I'm so sorry.

DEV
This is really intense.

GEORGE
I had no idea they were going to do this.

DEV
That was humiliating for me.

GEORGE
I know.

DEV
In front of your parents.

GEORGE
I know, but Jaqueline's on your side.

DEV
Felt like a-a horse having its hooves and flanks checked.

GEORGE
Listen, I hate to say it, but if that upset you, you're going to have to grow a thicker skin, because it's going to get a lot worse than that, okay?

Pause.

Are you ready for this? Because if you're not / ready for this—

DEV
I am. I'm ready.

Beat.

Are you?

GEORGE
Yeah, I am, but I've had a lot longer to prepare.

DEV
I just wanted to make a good impression.

GEORGE
You did.

DEV
I want you to know that it means so much to me that you invited me here.

GEORGE
I know it does.

DEV
And I'm scared shitless.

GEORGE
I know you are. But you're also the last person in the world who gives a damn about all this, you know, (*gestures at the room around him*) all this.

    Beat.

I can already tell they're impressed by you.

DEV
No.

GEORGE
They are.

DEV
They're thinking what a fucking liability.

GEORGE
Listen, there's going to be a lot of voices in the room, a lot of people saying a lot of things about us. But at the end of the day the only thing that matters is this.

    GEORGE *places one of his hands on his chest and the other on* DEV's *chest.* DEV *puts his hand over* GEORGE's *and nods.*

DEV
G-a-z-e.

    GEORGE *smiles.*

    They kiss.

    Lights shift.

PERFORMER 3
What I want to know is where the fuck is Astrid with those snacks?

PERFORMER 2
Yeah, girl.

PERFORMER 4
Astrid's sharing a fag with Charlotte and Sarah in the back garden is where she was.

PERFORMER 3
Dev is on good form through dinner, well-spoken as usual. The conversation is light and easy. No politics. Afterward there's brandy in the parlour and three rounds of something called the Hat Game—basically complex charades—which Dev and Charlotte win every round. Around midnight the boys say their good nights and retire to bed, George a little too drunk for sex, so they cuddle. George falls asleep and Dev lies there for a long time, listening to the sounds of the house at night.

Everything feels surreal, even the smell of the sheets. The feeling of George's hair on his cheek. Could this be my life, he thinks. He has grown up surrounded by images of this family, and yet what does he really know of them? And what could they possibly know of him, a twenty-four-year-old Asian British man? He wakes to the sound of people moving around downstairs, muffled conversation. It's already half past nine, they should hurry if they're going to make breakfast. He turns to George, and George's eyes are already open, fixed on him. He's in a playful mood.

Lights shift.

4.

Bedroom at Anmer Hall.

DEV *is fucking* GEORGE.

DEV
You like that?

GEORGE
Yeah.

DEV
You like me pounding your pussy like that?

GEORGE
Yes.

DEV
Yes what?

GEORGE
Yes sir.

DEV
Tell me what you like, boy.

GEORGE
I like your big dick in my pussy, sir.

DEV
Yeah?

GEORGE
Oh fuck.

DEV
You like that?

GEORGE
Oh fuck.

DEV
Lemme hear you moan.

GEORGE *moans.*

Good boy. Who owns your hole?

GEORGE
You do.

DEV
What?

GEORGE
You do, sir.

DEV
That's right.

GEORGE
Oh fuck. Fuck.

DEV
No no, hands off your dick.

GEORGE
Yes sir.

> DEV *stops fucking* GEORGE, *pulls out, and* GEORGE *turns around.*

(*quietly*) What's wrong, am I clean?

> DEV *doesn't respond as he's fishes in his bag and takes out a bottle of poppers.*

DEV
You want some?

GEORGE
Um. Okay. Yeah.

> DEV *extends the bottle toward* GEORGE*'s nose with one hand and uses his other to cover one of* GEORGE*'s nostrils.*

DEV
You gotta breathe in—there you go. Breathe in. That's it. Good. Fuck yes.

GEORGE
Whoa.

DEV
Yeah?

GEORGE
Ooof. Whoa.

GEORGE lies back.

DEV
Yeah? You good?

GEORGE
Fuck me.

DEV
Yeah?

GEORGE
Yeah. Pound my pussy.

DEV begins fucking GEORGE again, face to face.

DEV
You like being my little bitch?

GEORGE
Yes sir.

DEV
Fuck.

GEORGE
Yeah.

DEV
Fuck.

> DEV *places his hand around* GEORGE's *neck in a light chokehold.*

You like that?

GEORGE
Yes sir.

DEV
You my little bitch?

GEORGE
Yes sir. Fuck.

DEV
I'm close.

GEORGE
Yeah?

DEV
Oh fuck. Oh fuck.

GEORGE
Cum in me.

DEV
Yeah?

GEORGE
I want you to fucking / cum in me.

DEV
I'm cumming.

GEORGE
Oh my god.

DEV
Oh shit. Oh shit.

GEORGE
Yeah.

DEV
Oh shit.

DEV is spent. He gathers himself, looks down at GEORGE's chest.

Wait, did you come?

GEORGE
Yeah.

DEV
Just from me fucking you?

GEORGE
Yeah.

DEV
Oh wow.

GEORGE
Felt like I was cumming for two minutes.

They kiss.

DEV
What do you think your granddad would say about that?

GEORGE
What a lark!

DEV
Nothing he didn't see at Cambridge.

GEORGE
Don't even.

DEV
I bet your uncle Harry sucked a dick back in the day.

GEORGE
(exhales) I feel like I'm going to be sick.

DEV
Oh come on.

GEORGE
No, I mean my head's spinning.

DEV
It's the poppers.

> GEORGE *sits up, slings his legs over the side of the bed, and holds his head in his hands.*

GEORGE
Ooo boy, they really fucked me up.

DEV
You going to be okay?

GEORGE
I think I'm going to puke.

DEV
Really?

GEORGE
Yup.

GEORGE vomits.

DEV
Okay. All right. Lemme get a towel.

GEORGE vomits again.

Come to the toilet.

GEORGE
I'm good. I'm done. What?

DEV
You're such a chaotic bottom sometimes.

GEORGE
I don't think I like poppers.

DEV
And you liked wine after your first sip?

GEORGE
Are you my poppers sommelier?

DEV
I'll show you all the best vintages, babe.

DEV exits to the toilet to grab a towel. GEORGE gathers himself.

(off stage) Are they all white?

GEORGE
It's fine.

> DEV *returns with a towel and wipes up the vomit from the floor. With a facecloth he cleans* GEORGE *up a little too.*

DEV
Speaking of lingering stains on the monarchy.

GEORGE
Ha.

DEV
Now they're really going to love me.

GEORGE
They like you.

DEV
Yeah?

GEORGE
Definitely. Last night went well.

DEV
I get the feeling they're still a little unsure.

GEORGE
They're distant with everyone at first. My mum thinks you're very clever, she told me.

DEV
Maybe not the right kind of clever. Did you see how they glazed over when I was talking about Audre Lorde?

GEORGE
Because you were being boring.

DEV
Ms. Audre Lorde is never boring.

GEORGE
No, but her hype man sometimes is. They like that you're not from some posh aristo— Oh.

DEV
What?

GEORGE
You're coming out.

DEV
Uh oh—

GEORGE *starts shuffling to the toilet.*

Go sort yourself out, cub.

GEORGE *disappears off stage into the toilet.* DEV *begins changing back into his clothes and checks his watch.*

Shit, we gotta go. They're definitely done breakfast.

GEORGE
You checked any of the papers online yet?

DEV
Yeah, I had a peek last night.

GEORGE
And?

DEV
That picture of us is everywhere. I have about a hundred
WhatsApp messages.

GEORGE
Honestly, I feel relieved. I don't want it to be a secret anymore.
Your family know, right?

DEV
Yeah, yeah, I told them.

GEORGE
And what do they think?

DEV
They think it's a ludicrous fairy tale, which, of course, it is.

GEORGE
I'll have to meet them at some point.

DEV
Yeah, a little trip out to nasty-ass Barking.

GEORGE
I'd like to see where you grew up.

Sound of toilet flushing. GEORGE *emerges.*

What?

DEV
I'm just imagining you in my neighbourhood.

GEORGE
Oh come on.

DEV
What?

GEORGE
You think I'm such a ponce.

DEV
You are a ponce.

GEORGE
So are you.

DEV
Don't talk to your dom that way.

GEORGE
So are you always a dom?

DEV
With you I am.

GEORGE
Why, you wouldn't bottom for me?

DEV
You kidding? Getting fucked by the Prince of England? My ancestors would never forgive me.

GEORGE
But you've bottomed?

DEV
Baby, I'm doing a master's in the History of Art, of course I've bottomed.

They kiss.

You know what your parents are thinking? Shit, we've got another Meghan.

GEORGE *laughs.*

GEORGE
Yeah right.

DEV
I can guarantee it.

GEORGE
No.

DEV
The press will.

GEORGE *moves in close to* DEV. *They hold one another.*

GEORGE
Just try to relax.

DEV *nods.*

I know it's hard. What we're doing right now. This. This is big.

DEV
Yeah.

GEORGE
And I think it's going to hit us pretty soon just how big this is.
We've been sort of—in a bit of a bubble, haven't we?

DEV
Maybe you have. I think I've had a pretty clear idea how big
this is.

GEORGE
You can't just let the press get under your skin.

DEV
Right.

GEORGE
What?

DEV
That's easy for you to say.

GEORGE
In what way is that easy / for me to say?

DEV
Because you're protected. No matter what they say or do to you, at
the end of the day, you're still a prince. And at the end of the day,
I'm a Brown faggot.

GEORGE
I'm a fag too.

DEV
No, babe. You're not. You're a white gay prince. You will never be
a faggot.

GEORGE
O-kay.

DEV
Sorry.

GEORGE
So you just sort of dismiss my sexuality, or / whatever struggle that's
meant for me.

DEV
No, I'm not dismissing it, I'm offering you some perspective.

GEORGE
If you think this has been easy for me—

DEV
It has! Of course it has, it's been easier for you than literally any
human in the history of the world.

GEORGE
Well that's bullshit, I'm sorry.

DEV
And to be with you? Is like a suicide mission for me. I'm in the
plane right now, with my parachute, looking down at enemy fire.
The press is going to chew me up ten times worse than Diana or
Meghan, and meanwhile you'll just move on to the next thing
and on to the next thing, and long after I'm out of your life you're

going to be able to be a dozen, a hundred different things in their eyes—a prince, a philanthropist, a father, a king, a legend—and all I'll ever be is the Brown piece of ass you had at uni.

GEORGE
Why would you be out of my life? Don't, don't talk like that.

    DEV *smiles.*

What?

DEV
You can be so Disney sometimes.

GEORGE
What that's supposed to mean?

DEV
My Disney prince.

GEORGE
You calling me a romantic?

DEV
Something like that.

    Beat.

Speaking of which. I was going to give this to you later, but—

    DEV *fetches something out of his travelling bag. It's a small fabric bag tied with a ribbon.*

GEORGE
What is this, a bath bomb?

DEV
Yeah, I got you a bath bomb. Maybe you are a faggot.

DEV hands GEORGE the gift. GEORGE opens it.

GEORGE
Oh wow. What is this, a lion pin?

DEV
Yeah. Because you're my little lion cub.

GEORGE makes a growl and nestles into DEV.

GEORGE
I love it. I'm going to put it on right now.

DEV
Here.

DEV helps put the pin on GEORGE's shirt.

It's based on the lion from the Lion Pillar from Patna, in Bihar, where my father's family was from.

GEORGE
It's beautiful. Thank you.

DEV
The way its brow furrows like this reminds me of you.

They kiss.

All right, cub, let's do this. Round two.

Lights shift.

The performers begin changing costumes.

PERFORMER 3
When I first saw that scene in rehearsal I felt this . . . anger. I'm not sure if anger is the right word, but this—this overwhelming feeling of having been denied the experience of being a trans girl, like eighteen or whatever, and having just a normal first kiss, first crush, first romance. You know? Like, not sucking off some married man in his garage in the suburbs, or hearing about your friend getting their head caved in by a lead pipe. Having half your friends doing some form of sex work to pay for surgery in their twenties. And listen, this is not to say that I don't have a full and loving romantic life now, I do—I have a beautiful wife, friends, I love my life, my career, all that. And a part of me is like ugh I'm so done with queer tragedy. I'm exhausted by it. We have other stories. And then this other part, the part that watches that scene and still feels anger, still feels that—that wound, that part of me wants to tell George—you will never know that wound. You may think you know, but you will never know. And I resent that you'll never know. But I guess I'm also thankful that you'll never know. And you don't have to know, George, because people like me, people like me who came long before me, they were brave.

PERFORMER 4
They were brave in ways you will never have to be.

PERFORMER 3
Amen.

PERFORMER 4
Amen indeed.

PERFORMER 5
As news of Dev and George breaks, the Internet implodes.

PERFORMER 3
God save our little queen!

PERFORMER 4
Blow out that royal bussy, babe!

PERFORMER 2
Those boys are giving me hot flashes.

PERFORMER 3
Dev is our Diana!

PERFORMER 2
The fan fiction starts appearing immediately.

PERFORMER 5
Searches for the words "prince" and "royal couple" rise 500% on Pornhub.

PERFORMER 4
As do searches for "South Asian man" and "interracial."

PERFORMER 3
Naturally some of the discourse—

PERFORMER 5
Couldn't he find someone British?

PERFORMER 4
Glad someone's adding some spice to that Yorkshire pudding.

PERFORMER 2
Shouldn't he be driving an Uber?

PERFORMER 3
Well, you get the idea.

PERFORMER 4
Charlotte's friend Sarah has to return to London early, which leaves Dev alone with the royals for dinner on their second evening at Anmer. The conversation turns to George's appointment as the royal patron of the English National Ballet, and a recent remount he saw there of Pina Bausch's *The Rite of Spring*.

Lights shift.

5.

Dev, George, William, Kate, *and* Charlotte *at dinner.*

GEORGE
Yes yes but it also felt like pure ritual is what I am saying and I kept thinking—God, there are so few spaces for that in British life, or at least in my life.

CHARLOTTE
Are you kidding? Your life is entirely ritual.

GEORGE
Not like that. Not wild, and pagan, and-and bacchanal.

DEV
I don't know, I've seen you after a few negronis.

WILLIAM *laughs.*

GEORGE
When I was watching, I was just thinking—why am I sitting down? I should be up on that stage sweating, barefoot in that dirt.

CHARLOTTE
So why aren't you?

GEORGE
What?

CHARLOTTE
Why aren't you dancing anymore?

GEORGE
Well I think it's sort of obvious, no?

> CHARLOTTE *looks at* WILLIAM.

WILLIAM
What?

GEORGE
I think if I had been really excellent, like on track for the Royal Ballet School, then maybe you guys would have let me continue.

WILLIAM
We, hey, we never stopped you from dancing.

> GEORGE *takes a sip of his wine with his eyebrows raised.*

KATE
George.

DEV
Surely they would've let you into the Royal Ballet School if you'd auditioned?

GEORGE
No, I don't think so actually, and besides before I quit I was much more into contemporary anyway, and there was just no way I was going to be allowed to study that.

WILLIAM
Contemporary dance?

KATE
That was never even on the table.

GEORGE
I know, exactly.

DEV
How old were you? When you quit?

GEORGE
About fifteen.

WILLIAM
Where would you have even studied that?

GEORGE
I don't know, Trinity Laban maybe?

WILLIAM
Where?

CHARLOTTE
Dad.

WILLIAM
What?

CHARLOTTE
It's like a very famous school in London.

KATE
You're happy at Oxford.

GEORGE
Yeah I know.

KATE
And Dev wouldn't be here with us / if you hadn't gone—

CHARLOTTE
So you wouldn't have let him study contemporary dance?

WILLIAM
Sure, if he'd really wanted to.

GEORGE
Oh come on.

WILLIAM
If you had really been driven—

GEORGE
You're saying that you would've supported me through a degree in contemporary dance?

KATE
Well it's all academic now, isn't it?

CHARLOTTE
Or perhaps not academic enough.

GEORGE
Speaking honestly, you were both fine with the idea of a ballet prince. Right? That's respectable. But the moment I started doing contemporary it made you guys very uncomfortable, / it's fine to just admit it.

WILLIAM
No, I don't— I think that's a very revisionist way of how things went.

KATE
Dev, / did you ever—?

GEORGE
Mummy took me, I basically begged you to take me to see that
Florentina Holzinger show at Southbank, and you were horrified.

KATE
Oh come on, I was not.

GEORGE
You were, that sequence where they were naked with the candles
burning in their bums.

KATE
I thought that was quite funny, actually.

GEORGE
It wasn't meant to be funny, it was an allegory for rape, you didn't
even get that.

KATE
Excuse me?

WILLIAM
George, the point is—

GEORGE
You were embarrassed just being in the audience.

KATE
I wasn't embarrassed, / please, I'm not some prude.

WILLIAM
It was your choice to stop, we / never forced you to.

GEORGE
I didn't hear the end of it for making you see that show.

KATE
There are certain events, there are certain activities that are simply not suitable for royals, and that is one of the sacrifices we have to make.

CHARLOTTE
Yeah but who gets to decide what's suitable?

WILLIAM
Many people, Lottie, many factors.

KATE
I mean can you imagine the future king lying naked with a candle stuck in his bum at Sadler's Wells?

CHARLOTTE
I think that sounds brilliant. *(to DEV)* Don't you?

DEV
(smiling, shaking his head) I—

GEORGE
But ballet is fine.

KATE
Ballet—

GEORGE
Why? Because you think it's old-fashioned?

KATE
Well are you going to have a candle stuck up your bum in a ballet?

GEORGE
Maybe.

KATE
I doubt it.

CHARLOTTE
And so what? Why can't he?

KATE
We are not having this conversation.

CHARLOTTE
I just want to know why.

WILLIAM
Because there cannot be images of the future king in situations that many of his subjects would find compromising.

CHARLOTTE
But that's just their prejudice.

WILLIAM
Our job is to serve, not to make spectacles of ourselves.

CHARLOTTE
Not to make a spectacle / of ourselves, as royals?

WILLIAM
You know what I mean.

CHARLOTTE
With capes and crowns and motorcades, not to make a spectacle?

WILLIAM
There are some ways in which it is appropriate for a royal to be seen expressing themselves in public and some ways that are not, that is simply the case.

CHARLOTTE
And contemporary dance—?

KATE
A king should not be seen nude by his subjects, for one. No leader, / no politician—

GEORGE
Okay but, Mummy, we're not talking about nudity.

KATE
We are!

GEORGE
No, I get that I can't get naked in front of an audience, I'm not an idiot, but you know very well that no school, no dance school, was going to make me get naked, and still, regardless— *(stopping* KATE *from interjecting) Regardless*, it made you very uncomfortable in a way that ballet never did because it was weird, and artsy, and faggy, and that's what you're / not saying—it was too faggy.

WILLIAM
Do not use that word, and do not speak to your mother like that in front of a guest.

CHARLOTTE
Dev's family.

KATE
Dev is not family, with all due respect we have just met him, and the two of you better stop this right now.

CHARLOTTE
We've been asking perfectly legitimate questions.

GEORGE
Contemporary dance is the wrong kind of gay.

KATE
Who are you both trying to impress?

CHARLOTTE
Mum, we're adults. Okay? We might disagree with you.

KATE
You're barely seventeen, you are not an adult.

CHARLOTTE
Well seventeen is old enough for some things, just ask Uncle Andrew.

    An uncomfortable silence.

WILLIAM
I'm glad the coverage has been so favourable to you both.

CHARLOTTE
It's been two days.

WILLIAM
Well, it's important to get off on the right foot.

GEORGE
We've been mostly ignoring it.

WILLIAM
Good, that's for the best.

CHARLOTTE
Piers Morgan's tweet.

KATE
No.

GEORGE
What did he say?

> KATE *motions for* CHARLOTTE *to cut it out.* CHARLOTTE *turns to* GEORGE *and sticks her tongue suggestively in her cheek.*

KATE
Charlotte.

CHARLOTTE
What?

WILLIAM
Dev, I wanted to say, I was reading some of your essays—they're very good.

DEV
Oh wow, thank you. I appreciate you taking the time.

WILLIAM
Your parents must be very proud of you.

DEV
They are.

WILLIAM
George mentioned you're quite close with your father.

DEV
Yes. I am.

WILLIAM
And what does he make of all of this?

DEV
Well, uh—I think he's—

GEORGE
He's no fan of the crown.

DEV
I—

WILLIAM
He's not?

DEV
That's not true.

GEORGE
You told me yourself.

DEV
He's very happy for me, and I think mostly just apprehensive about
the scrutiny. It's impact on me, mostly.

GEORGE
He's very active in his community. Very political.

WILLIAM
Is he?

GEORGE
For the local Labour Party.

DEV
I can tell them myself.

WILLIAM
So you come by it honestly.

DEV
I suppose you could say.

WILLIAM
And he's open-minded, he's been supportive of your sexuality?

GEORGE
Why would you assume he isn't?

DEV
(to GEORGE) He's not.

WILLIAM
He's not been supportive?

DEV
(to WILLIAM) Oh no, no, he is. I just meant you weren't assuming.

GEORGE
Because he's Brown.

WILLIAM
What?

DEV
George—

GEORGE
He canvasses for Labour, of course he's supportive of gays.

DEV
I can speak for myself, thank you.

GEORGE
I know. I'm just saying—

DEV
I know what you're saying, please stop.

GEORGE
Okay, relax.

DEV
(*whispering to* GEORGE) I think you should relax, and I think you should stop drinking.

>   GEORGE *looks at* DEV. *A tense pause.* GEORGE *rises from his chair.*

GEORGE
Excuse me.

KATE
Where are you going?

GEORGE
The toilet. Or does someone need to accompany me there too?

GEORGE *exits.*

WILLIAM
We had a little disagreement before dinner, I think it may have set him off.

DEV
If I may ask, was it about me?

WILLIAM *exhales.*

WILLIAM
I wanted him to tell you personally but, uh . . . Kate and I and the Lord Chamberlain feel that, at least for the time being, while the news of the two of you is fresh, that you be accompanied by a security detail when you venture out in public together.

GEORGE *re-enters the room, clearly having listened from the hallway.*

GEORGE
So they can keep tabs on us.

KATE
It's not about keeping tabs.

WILLIAM
It's for your own safety.

GEORGE
And yet when you were both at St. Andrew's—

KATE
We're not getting into / this again.

GEORGE
Why don't you just station someone in our bedroom?

WILLIAM
I thought you needed the toilet.

GEORGE
This is a double standard, beyond protocol, because we're two men, / and I think it's completely unfair.

WILLIAM
It is for your own protection.

KATE
We're also living in a different time. / When the two of us were at uni—

GEORGE
Exactly, and we shouldn't have our every movement a-a-a-accompanied, and tracked, no couple can survive that!

GEORGE *storms back out. Pause.*

KATE
Are we ready for dessert?

Lights shift.

6.

DEV *is on his phone.*

DEV

Hi, Baba, yes, yes I'm here. We just finished dinner. What? A news crew? Outside the house? For how long? Well you can call the police and ask them to leave. Right. Okay. Well, you don't have to talk to them, you don't— No, I think it's best if you don't. Well unplug the phone. Just unplug it. It'll die down in a few days, I'm sure it will. I know. What do you mean threats, what kind of threats? Well just tell her not to read those comments. I can ask about a security detail, but that feels a little— Well I just don't know, it— Okay, I can ask. I'll ask. *(in Hindi) Kyonki mujhe voh bahut pasand hai Baba. Haan, mainne soch—Mainne socha tha aap par kya asar padega. Maaf kijiye Baba. Jo aap kehere voh teek nahi hain. [Because I really like him. Yes. I did—I did consider the impact on— I'm sorry. I don't think that's fair.]*

Baba, I'm sorry. I'm so sorry.

Lights shift.

PERFORMER 2

The royal press office would like the couple to keep a low profile, but instead they travel most weekends to London for art openings, premieres of plays, various fundraising galas.

PERFORMER 3

That's really Dev's influence.

PERFORMER 4
The two of them make acquaintances with the who's who of queer culture.

PERFORMER 1
But there are some things to which Dev never fully acclimates.

PERFORMER 2
Never being in charge of his own diary.

PERFORMER 3
"So from noon to quarter after twelve—"

PERFORMER 1
Dinners, receptions, speeches—

PERFORMER 2
Endless names to memorize.

PERFORMER 5
This is Prince Edward, Duke of Edinburgh, and his wife, Sophie, the Duchess, and their son James, the Earl of Wessex.

PERFORMER 4
And of course—

PERFORMER 2
Protocol.

PERFORMER 3
Protocol, protocol.

Libidinal techno plays.

Lights come up faintly on a private sex dungeon.

GEORGE is naked, gagged, blindfolded, and tied up in complex shibari bondage, suspended high above the space from hooks in the ceiling.

PERFORMER 5
Proper etiquette at the royal table—

PERFORMER 2
Thumb and index finger to hold the top of the teacup—

PERFORMER 3
—cutlery handles at the bottom right of the plate, like 4:20 on a clock—

PERFORMER 4
—wiping the upper lip with the inside fold of the napkin—

DEV slowly lowers GEORGE until he is only inches from the ground.

PERFORMER 5
The king sets the pace of every meal—

PERFORMER 2
—firm grasp, direct eye contact, two pumps, no more—

PERFORMER 4
—chin parallel to the ground and hands at your sides—

DEV caresses GEORGE's suspended body.

PERFORMER 5
—resting your hand on the banister, not grabbing—

PERFORMER 3

—simply push it to the back of the fork, *never* spear it—

DEV *bends down, removes the ball gag in* GEORGE's *mouth,
and kisses him, passionately. He then returns the ball gag to*
GEORGE's *mouth.*

PERFORMER 1

It's through being immersed in this life of endless ritual that Dev
understands something profound about his lover. That when all
you have ever known is a life of formality and power, you begin
to crave its opposite. The utter obliteration of the ego. One ritual
world for another.

Lights shift.

PERFORMER 3

Dev has hardly a spare hour to read anymore.

PERFORMER 2

Doesn't remember the last time he cooked a proper meal in his
own home.

PERFORMER 5

Can't just pop to the shop for some milk.

PERFORMER 4

His family and friends hounded.

PERFORMER 2

Constantly.

PERFORMER 3

Trailed by cameras to dinner, to the movies, to lectures—

PERFORMER 4
His phone is hacked twice.

PERFORMER 3
A childhood friend sells pen pal letters to *The Sun*.

PERFORMER 5
Grindr pics resurface.

PERFORMER 4
They weren't bad, to be honest.

PERFORMER 3
The press is relentless.

PERFORMER 2
"The wind reveals Dev's shocking receding hairline!"

PERFORMER 5
"Dev's Bombshell Views on Israel."

PERFORMER 3
"Dark Chatterjee Family Secret Revealed."

PERFORMER 4
And naturally, it's not long until —

> *Lights shift.* DEV *and* GEORGE *fight in* DEV's *Oxford post-graduate accommodation.*

DEV
Literal death threats, Cub —

GEORGE
I know, but —

DEV
Six this week in my Oxford inbox. Six! Where's the official state-
ment on that? Where's your mum and dad?

GEORGE
What would they say?

DEV
Anything!

GEORGE
I called Ted at *The Mail* on Friday / about the cartoon—

DEV
In *public*! In fucking public, where it counts! Where *they* can see!

 Lights shift.

PERFORMER 4
A constant sore spot is Dev's feeling that George never quite does
enough to stick up for him.

PERFORMER 3
Not to the press, or the public.

PERFORMER 5
Or to William and Kate.

PERFORMER 1
It eventually all comes to a head in their third year. Dev,
exhausted, feeling at the end of his rope, accepts a three-month
research residency in Genoa. He's excited to get away from it
all, the tabloids, the Firm, and, to be honest, away from George.
A least for a little while. He tells George he doesn't want to be

messaged. He needs to focus on his research. Just reading some books, doing a bit of writing. The space will do them good, he says.

PERFORMER 6
A break.

PERFORMER 1
A reset.

PERFORMER 6
George, reluctantly, agrees. What choice does he have?

PERFORMER 4
At first George finds the absence excruciating, but the pain gradually recedes into a dull ache. Like a phantom limb. The three months of the residency pass but Dev decides to travel to Venice for another two weeks, and then onto Rome. It's almost a full four months later that Dev is finally back in Oxford. On George's doorstep. In his arms.

7.

GEORGE *and* DEV *lie together in bed, naked.*

DEV
I heard from Rebecca that you've been going pretty hard while I've been away.

GEORGE
What's that supposed to mean?

DEV
At functions. Parties.

GEORGE
You're one to talk, Little Miss Ketamine.

DEV
Yeah but I know where to draw the line.

GEORGE
You don't think I know where to draw the line?

DEV
I think you know how to cut one with a credit card.

GEORGE *chuckles.*

GEORGE
It was so hard not messaging you. Drove me crazy the first few weeks.

Beat.

You know what I missed, more than anything?

DEV *looks at him.*

Your smell.

DEV
More than my conversation?

GEORGE
Yes.

They laugh.

DEV
The sweet scent of an exotic commoner.

GEORGE
It's not like that.

DEV
What's it like then?

GEORGE
When I think about your smell, I think about how—porous I am. That there are literally these particles of you that enter me, it reminds me that we're not self-contained units, but, like, miasmas of matter, / just these clouds, these storm fronts moving and crashing into one another.

DEV
Miasmas.

DEV *waits until the end of* GEORGE'*s line.*

I'm still very much in love with you, you know that, right?

GEORGE
It's never changed for me.

DEV
Some things need to change though, Cub. They can't go on as they have. I think you know that.

GEORGE
Well they won't.

DEV
Good.

GEORGE
Maybe not so good for you.

DEV
Why?

GEORGE *sighs.*

GEORGE
I'm doing a year with the army.

DEV *sits up.*

DEV
Wait, what?

GEORGE
I'm going to be head of the armed forces one day.

DEV
When, when did you —?

GEORGE
It's always been a thing.

DEV
So what does that entail? Guns?

GEORGE
Guns, yes.

  DEV *shakes his head.*

What?

DEV
I just assumed you'd be different.

GEORGE
What, that I'd be above civic duty?

DEV
Above proving your valour and worth through aligning yourself
with the / military-industrial complex.

GEORGE
Who do you think's sandbagging homes and rescuing people from
the floods right now? Sure as hell aren't gender theorists.

DEV
You can be damn sure if the government was giving gender
theorists seventy billion pounds a year we'd be up in Yorkshire
sandbagging too.

GEORGE
I knew you'd be like this.

DEV
Well, at least I'm consistent.

    Beat.

I really tried my best with you.

GEORGE
Please.

DEV
Doing shrooms in the woods, and reading Kwame Anthony
Appiah, and, and fucking bringing you to dinner with Ocean
Vuong, and now you're telling me that you're disappearing for a
year to run around with a bunch of gun-toting blokes to gain a bit
of street cred with the Greggs crowd?

GEORGE
Wow, listen to you, you've become a proper Oxbridge arse.

DEV
There are other symbols available to you.

GEORGE
It's not about symbols, it's about / real service, real duty.

DEV
Of course it's about symbols, you're not a real fucking soldier, George.

GEORGE
I want to be king.

DEV

Oh, I know you do.

GEORGE

And unlike you, I'm not cynical about the monarchy.

DEV

Well unlike you, I have a fucking reason to be.

GEORGE

My father, my grandfather, my great-grandmother, they've all been governed by a deep, a very, very deep sense of civic duty, and I am too. Do I have some, some ethical problems with the military, yes, of course. But I'm not so cynical like you about the people, the men and women who are willing to literally give up / their lives to serve our nation, and you can deconstruct this situation to within an inch of its life, but—

DEV

You think my reservations are rooted in cynicism. Wow. That's very interesting. I want you to just check in with the dynamic here, of who you are, and who I am, and ask me if my problems with the British military are rooted in cynicism.

DEV *smiles and shakes his head.*

GEORGE

What?

DEV

So you ask to get back together and then tell me I'm not going to see you for like a year.

GEORGE

Babe, you knew I had to do some service.

DEV
Yeah, I thought with, like, the coast guard or something.

GEORGE
It's all fine and well for you to be going to residencies, and conferences, and writing papers. I'm going to be king, Dev. You're going to be—

DEV
What?

GEORGE
I don't know.

DEV
Just a Brown subject.

GEORGE
A professor.

DEV
I will be a Brown subject in your kingdom, George.

> GEORGE *changes into his army uniform. The sound of a helicopter ascending.* GEORGE *looks up at the helicopter, in a callback to the original photograph of him at the age of four.*

PERFORMER 6
George, in his uniform, watches a military helicopter ascend into the sky. No longer clutching his face in wonder. But head shaved. Military fatigues. Heartbroken. He and his platoon evacuate stranded residents and their house pets after torrential rains in Northumberland. He slithers through the mud with an assault rifle. He shoots targets. As much as the army teaches George how

to fight, it also teaches him how to disassociate. Shirtless brawls. Busted lips. Puking guts. Snorting lines off his army-issue survival knife. Lads lads lads! He messages Dev erratically. Abusively. You worthless cunt. Dev blocks him. After his discharge, he returns to London. Spiralling.

Lights shift.

8.

A paramedic, played by PERFORMER 4, *helps* GEORGE *through a side door of the Kensington Palace apartments. The palace's head butler, Andrew* FARMER, *is there, awaiting their arrival.*

GEORGE
(to paramedic) Thanks, mate.

FARMER
Thank you, I've got him from here.

The paramedic exits.

GEORGE
I'm good, thanks, Farmer—I'm going to bed.

FARMER
George, I'm afraid that I have strict instructions from your father to detain you until his arrival.

GEORGE
Detain me?

FARMER
He's on his way.

GEORGE
Oh fuck. How're my pupils?

FARMER
Large.

GEORGE
What—what does he want? Who told him?

FARMER
I don't know the details.

GEORGE
I-I don't want to talk to him, I'm going to bed.

FARMER
Don't make this worse than it has to be. He'll be very upset with me if I let you go.

GEORGE *sighs, stays.*

GEORGE
Who the hell called—there was no need to call an ambulance.

FARMER
You were unconscious.

GEORGE
They could've, you know, splashed some water in my face.

FARMER
Who's they?

GEORGE
I'm not getting into it.

FARMER
Would you like some water?

GEORGE
No. Thanks. I just want to go to bed.

FARMER
Why don't you sit down.

GEORGE
I'd prefer to stand.

> GEORGE *stands for a moment, then sits down.* FARMER *sits down beside him.* GEORGE *leans his head against* FARMER's *shoulder.*

FARMER
You know, I used to do a lot of GHB when I was your age too.

> GEORGE *looks at* FARMER *for a moment and laughs.*

Do not breathe a word—

GEORGE
(*in a tone that suggests "Of course I won't"*) Farmer.

> *They both trace their fingers in the shape of a square.*

FARMER
In the vault.

GEORGE
In the vault.

FARMER
In my twenties I used to party with this group of gays that included this guy named Stephen Gately. Have you ever heard of the band Boyzone?

GEORGE *laughs.*

GEORGE
Boyzone? No.

FARMER
Well they were a huge deal back in the nineties. Legions of scream-
ing preteen girls, posters in bedrooms, that kind of thing. And
anyway, Stephen and his partner, who was also named Andrew,
and myself and a few other lads, we all went to Majorca on holiday
one time. And one night we all went to this club. And Stephen
goes into the dark room—

Just then ASTRID, *the servant, walks in.*

ASTRID
Sorry to interrupt, but Martin has a question about a delivery, sir.

FARMER
Thank you, dear, tell him I'll be right in.

ASTRID *exits.*

So Stephen meets this hunky young Bulgarian in this dark room—

GEORGE
(*playful*) Okaay.

FARMER
—and he and Andrew decide they want to have a threesome back
at their hotel room—

GEORGE
As you do.

FARMER

—so they say goodbye to us and leave. So doesn't Stephen take a bunch of GHB and passes out in bed almost immediately, which was very him, and the Bulgarian and Andy get it on, and then they fall asleep. The next morning Andy and the Bulgarian wake up, have sex again, right beside Stephen, and by this point it's almost noon and they finally think, oh maybe we should rouse him. Andy gives Stephen a little shake, and then a harder shake—

GEORGE

Oh no—

FARMER

—starts slapping him around the face, you know, come on, baby, wake up. Tries to give him mouth-to-mouth—

GEORGE

Did he choke on his vomit?

FARMER

No I don't think so, he just—I don't know, I don't actually know. The story the tabloids ran with was that he died of some congenital lung condition, which I'm sure was what his family was pushing. But all the queens knew the truth of course.

GEORGE

Shit.

FARMER

Indeed.

GEORGE

That is a war story.

FARMER
Learn from the parable of St. Stephen. Know your limits. And next time you're out partying in Soho, don't dismiss your SO1.

GEORGE
Well I wasn't going to take Pavol to the after-party.

FARMER
He's there for your protection.

GEORGE
How do you know I dismissed him?

FARMER
You went off the grid all weekend, George. You've caused quite a stir.

GEORGE *nods, processes this.*

GEORGE
You know who I saw out on Friday night? Dev.

FARMER
Your Dev?

GEORGE
He's not my Dev, he hasn't been my Dev in a year.

FARMER
So that's why you overdid it?

GEORGE
I don't know. Oh don't look at me like that.

FARMER
He was there with someone else, wasn't he?

GEORGE
Some agronomist, apparently.

FARMER
Heavens.

> WILLIAM *enters and* FARMER *stands.*

Your Royal Highness. I will leave you both.

WILLIAM
Good night, Andrew, thank you.

> FARMER *exits.*

Do you have any idea what a shitstorm you've created? Why haven't you replied to my texts?

GEORGE
I'm going to bed.

WILLIAM
George, one of the men you were with, at this party, took photos of you.

GEORGE
What?

WILLIAM
And I happen to have seen them. Though Jaqueline, who received them from Lachlan Murdoch, who was sent them by one of his editors, who received them from one of the charming men at your party.

> GEORGE *takes in the enormity of what his father has just said.*

GEORGE
Huh.

WILLIAM
Huh?

GEORGE
Can I see the photos?

WILLIAM
I don't have them on me, Jaqueline showed them to me on an iPad.

GEORGE *starts to smirk, suppressing a laugh.*

You find that funny?

GEORGE
Is it *The Mail*? Are they running the story?

WILLIAM
Of course they will, there's no point in killing it—if they don't do it, that friend of yours will sell it to someone else.

GEORGE *sighs.*

GEORGE
Fuck.

WILLIAM
His Royal Highness's chemsex weekend. I mean really. How stupid can you be? You were at a fucking party with other people, George, with phones and social media—

GEORGE
All the phones were taken and locked / in a box and hidden—

WILLIAM

Well clearly not all the phones! And then you gracefully extricate yourself by way of an ambulance at four thirty in the morning on a Sunday.

GEORGE

Well I'm sorry if the way I have sex, if my sexuality disgusts you.

WILLIAM

This has nothing to do with you being gay. It has everything / to do—well, first of all, with your safety, and second, with you being a royal, George.

GEORGE

Doesn't it?

WILLIAM

You're the heir to the fucking throne. Can you imagine if I'd been caught at a chemsex party?

> GEORGE *starts laughing at this. He cannot stop himself from laughing.*

Are you still high?

GEORGE

I didn't dress up as a Nazi! I didn't sleep with a seventeen-year-old girl.

WILLIAM

They're not heirs to the throne.

GEORGE

They're not faggots. That's my crime. Dressing up as a Nazi, hanging out with pedos, well that's just boys will be boys. Fucking some guys, minding my own goddamn business, that's / just immorality incarnate.

WILLIAM
Using illegal substances, George, is breaking the law.

GEORGE
I have sex the way I want and you hate that 'cause in your heart, deep down, it disgusts you, and scares you, like the old ladies at the fucking garden centres in the counties, well you all can go fuck yourselves.

  WILLIAM *takes a step toward* GEORGE *as if he might strike him.*

WILLIAM
Do not *ever* speak to me that way.

GEORGE
Talk to me when you're a gay man. Come back and / talk to me then.

WILLIAM
You are not just any gay man, George, / you're a—

GEORGE
And you're not one at all, so shut up.

WILLIAM
I don't recognize you right now.

GEORGE
Yourself, you don't recognize yourself in me. When this breaks tomorrow there're going to be hundreds of thousands of men around the world who recognize me, and recognize themselves—doctors, lawyers, bankers, teachers, famous fucking artists and

singers who you all love and praise and imagine, what, when they aren't teaching your kids or investing your money, go home and watch *Bake Off*? No. They're going and fucking each other in groups and yeah, maybe getting a bit high, and that is the unimaginable horror of faggots that you can't stomach. I'm not Mummy's sweet little mincing fawn anymore.

WILLIAM

You know your mother is so upset she doesn't want to speak to you right now.

GEORGE

Oh is she? Have I upset Mummy? And how about you? Running around with your fucking mistresses all my life, how do you / think that makes her feel?

WILLIAM

My what?

GEORGE

Did I mumble? And Mum's just supposed to grin and bear it.

WILLIAM

You have no idea what you're talking about—

GEORGE

Everyone knows, Dad, half of fucking Westminster knows you love getting pegged. Mom won't do it so you / find someone who will.

WILLIAM

THAT'S ENOUGH!

GEORGE

You love it up the arse just as much as me. Maybe Grandpa does too, you should ask him!

WILLIAM
You're still high. I can't talk to you like this.

GEORGE
No, truthfully, you can't talk truthfully, can you? You can't bear to really look at it. You'd prefer us to just spend our whole lives pretending not to know the things we do.

WILLIAM
Are you addicted?

> *This brings* GEORGE *up short.*

GEORGE
Sorry?

WILLIAM
Are you addicted? To crystal meth?

GEORGE
Oh is that the angle you're going to try to get Jaqueline to push? Rehab. Remorse. Rehabilitate / the image.

WILLIAM
I'm asking because I'm your father.

GEORGE
No.

> *Beat.*

I don't think so.

WILLIAM
You don't think so.

GEORGE
I don't . . . think . . . I am addicted, no.

WILLIAM
Is there a chance that you are?

GEORGE
I would say there is a chance that I am somewhere on the
spectrum.

WILLIAM
On the spectrum—

GEORGE
—of dependency, perhaps.

WILLIAM
Do you want to keep going to these parties?

GEORGE
I don't know how to answer that.

WILLIAM
A simple yes or no.

GEORGE
It's not a simple yes or no.

WILLIAM
So you don't have regrets about what happened. About the
emotional impact on me and / your mum and the rest of the
household.

GEORGE
Of course I do.

WILLIAM
But you would still consider / going to one of these —

GEORGE
Listen, I don't know what you want me to say.

WILLIAM
Would you be open to speaking to someone, professionally, about this?

GEORGE
You mean your PR team?

WILLIAM
You know what I mean.

GEORGE
Yeah okay. Maybe.

WILLIAM
Go and get some sleep. We have an eight a.m. crisis call with Jaqueline and Granddad.

GEORGE
I just want to say that I am literally the only gay man in this country who has to talk about chemsex with his granddad.

    GEORGE *begins to exit.* WILLIAM *grabs hold of him.*

WILLIAM
I love you.

    WILLIAM *is suddenly choked with emotion.*

I love you. And I'm worried about you.

GEORGE
Not as worried as you are about the press.

GEORGE *exits.*

After a moment KATE *walks in. She has been listening.*

WILLIAM
He's gone to bed.

KATE *shakes her head. She has tears in her eyes.*

KATE
How could he be so stupid?

Pause.

WILLIAM
Maybe we made a mistake.

KATE
No more than most parents.

WILLIAM
I mean with Dev. This wouldn't have happened if they were still together.

KATE
Are you mad?

WILLIAM
Dev grounded him, he gave / him a sense of responsibility—

KATE
He was the one who brought him to those awful parties!

WILLIAM
Not *those* parties. Different parties, not those ones.

KATE
We were right to force his hand. It had to end eventually. You know it did.

WILLIAM
It broke George's heart.

KATE
You think he's doing this to retaliate against us?

WILLIAM
Well —

KATE
There's no way George knows.

WILLIAM
That we had the Lord Chamberlain speak with Dev?

KATE
He doesn't know.

WILLIAM
He may find out one day.

KATE
Well, let him hate us for it then.

WILLIAM
I'm just worried for my boy.

KATE

He needs help, professional help.

WILLIAM

But there's not a rehab facility in this country I would trust with security, with leaks.

KATE

We do it in-house, then, with our own doctors.

WILLIAM

Hmm. Balmoral perhaps. Somewhere remote.

KATE

Are we certain it's addiction?

WILLIAM

I saw him, I'm positive.

KATE

He's always had this— I don't know what you'd call it. Do you remember when he was maybe four or five and I told him not to put his tongue on that—that frozen railing and he did it right away. Like he was testing me.

WILLIAM

No, see—? He wasn't testing you. He was testing himself.

KATE *consider this.*

KATE

Even as a boy. He always wanted more. More attention, more cuddles, as a boy, more pushes on the swing, just one more, one more story before bed, one more kiss, one . . . *(She wells up.)* Just one more kiss, Mummy, please.

WILLIAM
But you did kiss him.

KATE
Of course I did.

WILLIAM
Well that's not a given in this family.

KATE
Your mother did.

WILLIAM
Of course she did. But if I'm honest, I don't remember them anymore. Her kisses. If she told me stories. I'm sure she must have. But. I have no memory of it anymore.

KATE
When I see him I still see that boy, always wanting one more push.

WILLIAM
Well. Let's help give him the push he needs.

Lights shift. PERFORMER 2 *is alone on stage as he begins to undress and change costume.*

PERFORMER 2
Okay, so. I played Henry v in university. And I'll never forget, I'd just done this speech in rehearsal, the one where he's rousing the men before Agincourt, and the director of the show, who was a teacher of mine, told me that he wanted me to do it again, but to take some of the gangster swagger out of it. I was like, I'm sorry what? And he sort of caught himself and used other words, but I knew what he was saying. He was saying: I need you to take some of the Black out of it. "He has to be noble, but not cocky." I was

like—right. I was super defensive at the time. I thought to myself, you want me to just copy Sidney Poitier? Can it only be one thing? What is a Black king? Who are the Black men of power in this world? Don't tell me for a fucking second what a Black king looks like. Sometimes I think about my old teacher sitting out there, watching this. You know. Buying a ticket. Coming to the theatre. Opening the program, and, oh wow, maybe didn't realize I was in it, maybe he's feeling some pride, "That's one of mine." And then we get to this part of the show. I stiffen the sinews, summon up the blood. And I look out into the audience, and oh my god I see him, I see him there. And I look toward him. And I just say: Fuck you. Fuck. You. *This* is what a Black king looks like.

Lights shift.

PERFORMER 1
The year is 2044. George is now thirty. King Charles III is dead. Long live King William V.

Lights shift.

9.

A room in Windsor Castle. GEORGE *and* CHARLOTTE *are in formal funeral wear.* CHARLOTTE *is pouring them both whiskies.*

CHARLOTTE
When I die, there's going to be no funeral, no procession, no lying in state or any of that crap. I just want to have a Tibetan-style sky burial.

GEORGE *laughs.*

You know? Like, lay my body out in Hyde Park and let the gulls pick me apart.

CHARLOTTE *hands* GEORGE *a drink. She raises her glass.*

To Grandpa.

GEORGE
To Grandpa.

CHARLOTTE
I hope he gets reincarnated as an orchid.

GEORGE
He would love that.

CHARLOTTE
You know, as frustrating as he could be at times, he really was quite a gentle soul, wasn't he?

GEORGE
I was always such a disappointment to him.

CHARLOTTE
No.

GEORGE
I know I was.

CHARLOTTE
He saw you through a really hard time.

GEORGE
Mmm.

CHARLOTTE
He loved you.

 Beat.

GEORGE
It's funny, one night when he was in hospital, it was just Daddy and me in the room, he asked me how Dev was getting on.

CHARLOTTE
Oh no, poor guy. He was really slipping at the end.

GEORGE
Yeah but then, the thing is, I actually ran into Dev just last week.

CHARLOTTE
Really?

GEORGE
At the ballet, yeah.

CHARLOTTE
I haven't thought about him in years.

GEORGE
You know what Mum asked me once, during that first weekend at Anmer?

CHARLOTTE
What, how big's his dick?

GEORGE
Oh my god can you imagine?

CHARLOTTE
(*imitating* KATE) Go on, tell me, Georgie. Just between us, how big?

GEORGE
(*imitating* KATE) Just between us girls.

They're laughing.

No but seriously she came up to me after dinner and asked, "Do you—" No wait, what was the exact wording? She was like, "Do you think it's a fit?"

CHARLOTTE
See, she was asking about his dick.

GEORGE
Like, she wasn't asking if he was a fit romantically. You know?

CHARLOTTE *nods.*

CHARLOTTE
I know.

GEORGE
Was he a fit for this?

 GEORGE *gestures around him.*

That was, like, literally her first question.

 CHARLOTTE *nods.*

It's too bad you didn't get to spend more time with Dev, I think you two would've really got on.

CHARLOTTE
I've always liked him.

GEORGE
The looks he'd give me during official nonsense, like even just some of the ceremonies at Oxford, he—

 GEORGE *chuckles.*

He was so good at taking the piss out of things. He could always see things for what they were.

CHARLOTTE
Grandma asked me again today whether there was a man in my sights.

GEORGE
I like how she always makes it sound like big-game hunting.

CHARLOTTE
Didn't ask me about the foundation, or the work at the British Museum, no. For her the things I'm involved in are, like, fun window dressing around my real job, which is to be a kind of

beautiful void. That's all people really want from me, is to show up, smile, be a hanger for clothes, a womb for babies. And honestly? Mum did the job beautifully. She's the perfect royal. I love her, but she's fantastically ordinary, completely unchallenging, not an intellectual, not—

    KATE *and* WILLIAM *enter.*

KATE
There you are.

    CHARLOTTE *and* GEORGE *stub out their cigarettes.*

Not in the palace, please.

WILLIAM
Is Louis not with you?

    A subtle light shift.

PERFORMER 4
Yeah, where the hell is Louis in this play?

PERFORMER 3
Who cares!

PERFORMER 2
Poor Louis.

    A subtle light shift, return to the previous state.

KATE
It stinks of smoke in here, open another window would you?

GEORGE *opens a second window while* WILLIAM *fixes himself and* KATE *a drink.*

GEORGE
Has Nanna left?

KATE
I don't know, dear, did you say goodbye to Camilla?

WILLIAM
Did you not?

KATE
No.

WILLIAM
It's fine, we're seeing her tomorrow.

KATE
She was so strong all day, wasn't she?

CHARLOTTE
Please, please stop equating stoicism with strength, Mum.

KATE
But she was—

CHARLOTTE
She was stoic. She didn't cry. That doesn't mean she was strong, or weak.

KATE
The public expect a certain decorum.

CHARLOTTE
And she delivered.

KATE
Yes, which takes immense self-control.

> CHARLOTTE *and* GEORGE *exchange a look.* WILLIAM *hands* KATE *her drink.*

Oh, thank you.

> WILLIAM *sits down.*

WILLIAM
Oh my god.

KATE
You must be exhausted.

> WILLIAM *nods.*

Well it went smoothly. It didn't rain.

> WILLIAM *raises aloft his glass.*

WILLIAM
Here's to Pa.

KATE
To Pa.

> *The four of them toast.*

WILLIAM
May Mum forgive him when they meet.

CHARLOTTE *and* GEORGE *share a glance as they all take a drink.*

WILLIAM *turns to* GEORGE *and* CHARLOTTE.

How are you two holding up?

GEORGE
Good.

CHARLOTTE
Yeah. Feeling "strong."

WILLIAM
George, your mum and I were talking earlier —

KATE
We don't have to —

WILLIAM
What?

KATE *shrugs, gestures for him to proceed.*

We were talking about how with the coronation now, and your investiture in Wales, and the possibility of an election, and the Olympics, how . . . perhaps . . . it would be best to hold off on the wedding until next summer.

GEORGE
Oh. 'Kay.

WILLIAM
As a thought.

GEORGE
Is that what Jaqueline suggested?

KATE
It was my suggestion, actually.

WILLIAM
Jaqueline agrees.

KATE
As do you.

WILLIAM
As do I.

GEORGE
Well it seems settled then.

KATE
No, we wanted to consult you and gauge your reaction.

GEORGE
What did you think my reaction would be?

KATE
Well, I hope you'd be gracious about it and consider the bigger picture.

GEORGE
Thom and I want to start a family.

KATE
We know.

GEORGE
So— So I don't know what to say.

    Beat.

He's going to be very disappointed.

KATE
I know.

WILLIAM
We're all disappointed.

GEORGE
We knew Grandpa was going to die, I don't see how this is news.

KATE
I think it's just becoming clear that the year's going to be too busy.

GEORGE
I hate the Olympics so much—

CHARLOTTE
I can't believe you're / fucking up his wedding.

KATE
It's not / just the Olympics—

GEORGE
And I am not, we have gone over this, doing some large investiture ceremony at Carnarvon.

WILLIAM
We're not talking about that right now.

CHARLOTTE
I think that's really misjudging the mood.

WILLIAM
We're not getting into it.

GEORGE
Well, I don't think I have a lot of say in the matter, so I might as well call Thom and let him know.

KATE
We don't have to make a decision tonight.

GEORGE
The decision clearly has already been made. I feel like it's only polite to let him know as soon as possible.

WILLIAM
Can we just sit as a family for a few moments?

GEORGE *is collecting his things.*

KATE
George, please.

WILLIAM
Just sit down.

GEORGE
I'll see you all in the morning.

WILLIAM
I said *sit down.*

GEORGE *stops and looks at* WILLIAM.

GEORGE

I heard what you said. You don't need to say it louder.

WILLIAM

Tonight is not about you.

GEORGE

No, I know, it's about you. And so is this year, and next year, and every other year until it's you we're sticking in that fucking chapel. Thom and I've invested a lot of time and energy into this now. A lot of-of emotional energy. It's been keeping us going. But whatever. It's fine. It doesn't matter. We'll do the wedding next year.

Lights shift.

10.

PERFORMER 4

2044, smart roads and self-driving cars are the norm, and yet no fewer traffic jams and accidents. Little genetically modified tigers the size of house cats are becoming all the rage in Japan.

PERFORMER 3

Parents will go to any length to give their children genetic advantages. Some countries have started regulating against it, others are providing state funding for it.

PERFORMER 2

The lives of the wealthy continue to get longer. While widespread droughts and famines lead to mass migration and civil unrest.

PERFORMER 5

The rain, however, continues to fall in London.

Lights shift.

GEORGE *is standing in the rain, talking with* DEV. DEV *holds an umbrella.*

DEV

(*calling off stage*) I'll catch up, go on. Yeah, yeah, I'll meet you there.

GEORGE

Who're they?

DEV
Just some friends, listen what the hell are you doing? You can't just jump out of a car at me, I thought I was being mugged.

GEORGE
I know, I—

DEV
How long have you had your driver tailing me?

GEORGE
I was just on my way past, and I saw you and I had him turn around. And then we followed you for a couple of minutes.

DEV
Are you drunk?

GEORGE
I can't believe that's your first question.

DEV
It's not, it's my third question.

GEORGE
Why would you assume that?

DEV
Because you seem drunk.

GEORGE
I'm a little.

DEV
George—

GEORGE
I miss you.

DEV
What?

GEORGE
Seeing you the other night, at the ballet, I realized—I—I'm not
with the right person.

DEV
I'm sorry to hear that. But that's not my problem.

GEORGE
And you, are you with the right person?

DEV
I mean I love Miguel, yes.

GEORGE
He seems very impressive.

DEV
He is.

GEORGE
And Thom is—

DEV
He seems very . . . nice.

GEORGE
Oof. Damning.

DEV
And precisely my opposite.

GEORGE
You're not nice?

DEV
No. Not chiefly.

GEORGE
We're getting married next year.

DEV
Wow. Okay.

GEORGE
Yeah.

DEV
Congratulations.

GEORGE
We've been trying not to talk about it. Don't mention it / to anyone, obviously.

DEV
No, no.

 Beat.

You and your child bride.

GEORGE
He's not that much younger than me.

DEV
Six years?

GEORGE
Five.

DEV
Does he keep his pinky finger out when he fists you?

GEORGE
He's not some ponce.

DEV
Does he know what a filthy pig you are?

GEORGE
We're exploring.

DEV
So what, he pinches your nipples sometimes?

GEORGE
He's a very good lover.

DEV
I'm sure he is.

GEORGE
As were you.

DEV
I know.

GEORGE

He was incredibly intimidated by you, I don't know if you could tell.

DEV

I could tell. Why don't you have an umbrella?

GEORGE

I don't know, I don't carry my own.

DEV extends his umbrella and GEORGE steps under it.

DEV

I don't know what you're hoping to-to get out of this—

GEORGE

When I saw you the other night, I realized, I love you. I never stopped loving you.

DEV

And yet, George, I'm probably the one homosexual in the world who doesn't want to be your partner.

GEORGE

Why?

DEV

What do you mean why, we have partners.

GEORGE

I know, but in theory—

DEV

In theory what?

GEORGE *begins to cry.*

GEORGE
In theory— In theory do you still think about me? I mean— In
theory—

DEV *looks around. He puts a hand on* GEORGE'S *shoulder.*

DEV
George, you're drunk, you gotta pull yourself together. I don't want
to be photographed with you crying like this.

GEORGE
Are you embarrassed?

DEV
No, I just don't need another / smear piece to—

GEORGE
You're literally embarrassed by me.

DEV
—to burnish my reputation among your family and fans. What did
your grandfather call me again?

GEORGE
He said you were my Master of the Dark Arts.

DEV
Right. I'm sure he meant to say your Darkie with a Master of Arts.

GEORGE *laughs in spite of himself.*

GEORGE

Would you be open to spending some time together? Like a weekend or something?

DEV

George, this feels really desperate. You jumping out / at me like
this in the street.

GEORGE

Because it is. I am. You make me feel desperate. Do you still love
me, at all?

DEV

Of course I do, but—

I will never be allowed to be your partner. The powers—

GEORGE

What are you / talking about?

DEV

Let me finish. The powers that be, and you know what I'm talking
about, will never let me be your partner, and you know, somewhere deep down, you know that's true. And it is too painful and
too damaging for me to consider that possibility. So I let it go. A
long time ago. And you need to too.

GEORGE

Well I won't.

DEV

The sooner you do, the better off you'll be.

GEORGE
Do you want to see *Idomeneo* with me tomorrow night?

DEV
I need to go.

GEORGE
No, no, no.

DEV
You know where I'm off to now? I'm on my way to a renters' union meeting. And you? You're getting a drive back to Kensington Palace, I mean the cognitive dissonance of me / talking to you here—

GEORGE
But I could come with you.

DEV
You can't!

GEORGE
I'm not saying that I will, but there's / no reason why I couldn't—

DEV
We don't live in the same world, we never have and we never will.

GEORGE
But I want to.

DEV
You don't. You say you do, but you'll do nothing to actually change the course that you're on. In any real, fundamental way, you won't. Look. What you need to understand, George, what after all of these years you still don't seem to get, is that there is some queerness that

is permissible and has always been permissible within the halls of power, and that is your kind. Do you think you'll be the first gay king of England—?

GEORGE
I mean—

DEV
You won't.

GEORGE
But—

DEV
And there are some kinds of queerness that will never really be allowed in through the front door. Maybe it can sneak in through the back, from time to time, but mostly it's kept on the curb where it belongs. And here I am, on the curb. In the rain. And I don't feel sorry for myself in the least. Because I am part of something far more profound than you will ever be—

GEORGE
Yes, but—

DEV
That you will never be a part of. And I know you want to be of this family. But you can't. Not as long as you're a fucking royal. The divinely anointed head of the Church of England. The literal embodiment of empire.

GEORGE
I think what you're saying is really fucked up and / kind of problematic, actually—

DEV
You don't get to colonize three quarters of the world, brutally sub-
jugate millions of people, and then ponce around with a crown a
century later and pretend we forgive—we don't. We don't forgive you.

GEORGE
You don't forgive me?

DEV
You have inherited palaces, and riches, and fame, but you also
inherited / blood, and it is on your hands.

GEORGE
Palaces and riches *you* enjoyed, you fucking hypocrite.

DEV
I put up with it for you.

GEORGE
You're so full of bullshit. So that's it? There's no way that I can ever
be part of "your family" as you call it.

DEV
I mean . . . you could walk away.

GEORGE
What?

DEV
Just walk away.

GEORGE
Renounce the crown?

DEV *raises and drops his arms.*

You serious?

Beat.

That would be completely—

DEV
It would be completely legendary. You could throw your lot in on
the side of the oppressed. You could say, you know what? Maybe
there shouldn't be a hereditary monarch in the twenty-first century.
Maybe, maybe we could give back some of these stolen jewels and
pieces of furniture, which were made with slave labour, and we /
could start offering reparations to the victims—

GEORGE
Oh my *goddd*! So you want to be right instead of happy? You're
shouting fucking theory at me on the street, who do you think you
are, you're not a fucking anarchist, you're not some Marxist revolu-
tionary, you teach at LSE and have a fucking Equinox membership.
I just think it's totally crazy that we can't be together because of
the-the Mau Mau Uprising or something!

DEV
You don't get it.

GEORGE
I don't, I guess. I mean I do, theoretically, but love doesn't— I just
don't see how you can deny feelings like that, rationalize your way
out of something we both feel, I think it's mad.

DEV
I'm sorry we're having this conversation like this, in the rain, this
wasn't my intention.

GEORGE
Was it your intention to ever have this conversation?

DEV
I don't know. I'd be lying if I said I hadn't dreamt of it.

GEORGE
I bet this feels really good for you.

DEV
I'm not sure I would use the word "good," but . . .

DEV *suddenly notices the lion pin on* GEORGE*'s shirt.*

Is that—?

GEORGE
What?

DEV
The lion pin.

GEORGE
Oh. Yeah.

DEV
I didn't realize you still wore it.

GEORGE
I don't often. It must have summoned you.

DEV
Yeah. Right. The ancient magic of Ashoka.

GEORGE
So just-just to be clear—

DEV
I think I've been pretty clear.

GEORGE
—you're saying you would consider getting back with me if I gave up the throne. Is that literally what you're saying?

DEV
Yeah. I guess that's literally what I'm saying.

Lights shift.

11.

Low lighting, almost like a seance.

GEORGE *pulls off his clothes until he is naked. He is crying and drunkenly mumbling to himself.*

The other performers don costumes of EDWARD II, RICHARD *the Lionheart, Queen* ANNE, *and King* JAMES I.

PERFORMER 2
George arrives home soaking wet.

PERFORMER 3
Shivering.

PERFORMER 2
Two o'clock in the morning.

GEORGE
You're getting married, goddammit.

PERFORMER 5
Is love just a kind of madness?

PERFORMER 2
A mania?

GEORGE
He's just a man, you don't give up the throne— For what?
For love?

PERFORMER 4
What will cure him of Dev?

GEORGE
How could he even ask that?

PERFORMER 4
The only man he's ever really loved.

GEORGE
No, no, no shut up shut up!

He starts hitting his head.

You're happy with Thom, Thom is good, he's decent, just focus on the wedding, goddammit.

PERFORMER 3
George takes a tab of acid.

GEORGE
Shhhh —

PERFORMER 4
Then another.

GEORGE
Only candles
A dark, cavernous room
Surrounded by the dead
Everywhere in this castle dead, dead, *dead*
A room of portraits
Edward the Second
My god
Richard the Lionheart

He moves
Queen Anne
No, no, no
King James
Get back!
Stay where you are!

JAMES I
The great buggers of the English crown!

ANNE
And a daughter of Sappho.

GEORGE
Please, please, please don't come any closer—

> As the lights continue to darken, the sound of GEORGE's
> heartbeat begins to fill the space.

ANNE
Poor boy, look at you

JAMES I
A terrible choice you have before you, George
Between love and country

EDWARD II
Come to your senses, child

JAMES I
The crown!

RICHARD
You can't let some passing fancy knock you off course

GEORGE
What do you know? So what, you're buggers, any king can fuck a soldier or a page boy. But what do you know of love?

EDWARD II
Surely you don't love this commoner?

GEORGE
But I do, I do, I never stopped.

ANNE
And you desire some kind of life with him?

GEORGE
Yes.

JAMES I
Where would you even live?

GEORGE
I don't know, in a—house in Cambridge, say. And he could bike into town and teach his classes, and work on / his book in the evenings in the study, and I would, I don't know—

ANNE
Oh George . . .

JAMES I
(*replying to end of* GEORGE's *line*) Exactly, what would you do?

GEORGE
I would busy myself, I'd read, I'd cook, / and visit friends, and travel, and be a loving partner. I mean, doesn't that sound like a good life?

JAMES I
Cook!

JAMES I waits until the end of GEORGE'S *line.*

George, you have a good life.

GEORGE
But he doesn't want it!

RICHARD
My boy, we have watched you from birth, we know your desires, your ambitions—

JAMES I
And trust me, George, unlike your father, you have true vision, you have real ideas about the way we live in the world that—

GEORGE
And by the time he dies I'll be ancient, I'll be lucky if I can chew my own food! I can't bear to be like my grandpa, waiting / and waiting and waiting until I'm eighty, for what?

EDWARD II
George, one day you are going to be king. You would give that up for some sodomite of low birth?

JAMES I
You mustn't be afraid of greatness. The crown, George, is—

GEORGE
—is a crown of blood! Dev's right why should I even want it?

ANNE
Because you are not just some sodomite!

GEORGE
Yes, I am!

ANNE
You're a prince!

GEORGE
I'm a faggot!

RICHARD
You're a dog!

GEORGE
Rather be a dog than a tyrant. Than a butcher. Blood on my hands.
Black blood. Blood of witches. Of sodomites. My own blood, on
my own hands. Damn you. Damn damn damn all of you.

GEORGE *breaks down.*

I've fucked it up. I need to go back. No, no, no. Black holes.
Idomeneo. And his eyes. His eyes. Black holes. On the curb. Listen.
No, no, stop, what are you doing—?

ANNE
It's your acid trip, dear.

GEORGE
I need—

EDWARD II
What, what do you need?

GEORGE
To feel, to know, to know everything I could be, everything
I could feel, desire, I have such desire, things I want to do

with my body, to become, that I could never, I mean places, people— Just to cruise, to kiss, to fuck, to turn myself inside out, even just to go to a club, to dance, to feel Dev's sweat, his back against my chest, holding him, clasped together, moving in the black, his black eyes, lips, bodies all around us, and you think *oh so what*, but what is this if not the most intimate and essential, I mean *spiritual*—the taste of leather, handcuffs, boot on my throat, licking the sole, my soul— How do I transcend myself? Just to leave this, all this, my body, the weight, the weight of everything, I mean do you have any idea how much I want to be tied up? Tied down. Strapped to a bed or a-a-a metal table with a ball gag in my mouth. I want to feel it all. I want to—

Queen ANNE *pulls a latex dog hood over* GEORGE's *head and affixes a leash to him.*

EDWARD II *sticks a dildo dog tail into* GEORGE's *ass.*

Techno is now pounding. Strobes and haze.

GEORGE *is at a rave.*

The other performers change out of their royal clothing and return to being themselves.

PERFORMER 1 *enters in white face and period garb and grabs* GEORGE's *leash.* GEORGE *moves down to the ground, doglike.* PERFORMER 1 *leads* GEORGE *away, still in the dog mask.*

PERFORMER 5 *begins to disrobe from his royal garments.*

After a long moment:

PERFORMER 5

I had this friend who said to me once, this was back in the late eight-
ies and we were having a drink after a show, and she said—David,
you have to let me teach you how to be fisted. And I said—Pardon?
No thank you. Then she took my hands and she said, David, look,
you have very small hands, you would be very popular. You should
come to my workshops. She had just begun teaching these fisting workshops with her girlfriend at the Mineshaft—I'm not even
joking—to gay men on Saturday afternoons like it was a community
centre, and they'd have Arrowroot cookies and apple juice. And she
said to me, I'm doing it because I'm sick of all my friends dying.

That year I held five different friends' hands as they died.

You had people like Larry Kramer shouting, "You faggots have got
to stop having sex. You just have to *stop*." Well no one was stopping, I mean some people did, I did, to an extent, I—got married,
eventually, which was one way to survive, I guess. The thing I think
some people forget, or maybe don't even realize, is that fetish—the
leather, the latex, the BDSM, fisting—I mean it was on some very
fundamental level about survival. About decentring the penis as
the-the sole focus of sex.

The thing that nobody tells you, my friend continued as were
sitting at the bar, is that when you're fisting someone, you can feel
their heartbeat. Around your hand. And I thought . . . I'll never
forget her saying that . . . I thought . . . Oh now that. *That* is something I think I *would* enjoy feeling. A heartbeat. Against my hand.

    PERFORMER 5 raises his hands.

Against my very small hands.

    Lights shift.

12.

PERFORMER 2

The year is 2045. The singularity is almost upon us. Brad Pitt dies
alongside eleven others on Elon Musk's first manned flight to
Mars. The world has grown more religious. Some countries are
rocked by anti-science movements. Including this one. We wage
war over past recriminations. Imaginary enemies. Dev's words
linger with George. George, in turn, begins to write Dev, a new
letter every week. Until, at the end of the year, Britain celebrates its
first gay royal wedding.

Lights shift.

Sounds of a massive crowd cheering. Orchestral music.

Two performers become television royal correspondents.

Meanwhile, the other performers begin dressing DEV *in
a tuxedo, including vest, white bow tie, and tails. This
dressing is the main action taking place while the royal correspondents speak.*

CORRESPONDENT 1

We have a commoner marrying the next in line to the throne, so
the mix inside Westminster Abbey this afternoon is quite something.
Over a thousand friends. Do you have a thousand friends, Richard?

CORRESPONDENT 2

I'm afraid I'm a few shy.

CORRESPONDENT 1 *chuckles.*

CORRESPONDENT 1
Me too.

CORRESPONDENT 2
Oh, and here we go, here comes Prince George and his best man, Prince Louis, in their car now. Looking calm. Looking content. Acknowledging the crowd very happily.

CORRESPONDENT 1
I'm told reliably that Prince Louis does have the ring in his possession, and he's carrying it to the abbey. It's a great sight. The expanse of the mall.

CORRESPONDENT 2
And now continuing down Whitehall, where the crowds began gathering at five o'clock this morning, past Downing Street, where there will be a street party later on.

CORRESPONDENT 1
You can hear now the bells of the abbey ringing out as Prince George arrives and steps out from his black Aston Martin, the very same car his father rode in on his wedding day.

Lights appear on Prince GEORGE. *He is at a distance, far up stage, with his back to us. He is regally dressed in his military uniform.*

CORRESPONDENT 2
And there we have—a better view, really, of the man of the hour, well one of two men of the hour, Prince George. The other of course being his groom, Aubrey Thomas Ashberry. Known to his friends and family as Thom.

At this moment, the other performers stop dressing DEV, *and stand behind him. The music begins to fade away.*

CORRESPONDENT 1
For many watching at home, Richard, after so many decades, this must feel like something of an endgame, does it not, for the LGBT struggle for rights and visibility?

CORRESPONDENT 2
Very much so, yes.

CORRESPONDENT 1
To live to see this happen, here today in Westminster Abbey—

A sudden shift—lower lights on everyone except a spot on DEV *and a fainter spot on* GEORGE.

DEV
Did you think, perhaps, for a moment that this was my wedding? Or maybe you thought I was invited. No. I am not even in the abbey. I am not among the thousand. I am not among the chosen. Those without money are not chosen. We do not sing the hymns. We do not rub shoulders. I have, however, been invited to a party at the university to mark the occasion. I put on a nice suit. And I go. Because I would rather do this than sit alone, in my house. And at this party, this function, there is a television. And as I watch—

The correspondents are now faintly lit. As they speak GEORGE *slowly turns around to face out toward the audience.*

CORRESPONDENT 1
Doesn't the prince look regal?

CORRESPONDENT 2
He does indeed.

CORRESPONDENT 1

He is in the frock coat uniform of the Blues and Royals. On the
left breast he is wearing a Pilots Wings badge for serving in the
Army Air Corps. Next to that is the Star of the Grand Cross Knight
Commander of the Royal Victorian Order.

CORRESPONDENT 2

And what is that on his right breast? Do you see that?

CORRESPONDENT 1

Yes, it appears to be some kind of gold pin.

CORRESPONDENT 2

It looks like a lion's head.

CORRESPONDENT 1

I think you're right, yes, it's a—gold lion pin. I don't have that in
my notes, I'm not sure. Trust the prince to add a dash of whimsy
though, to every occasion.

Lights fade out entirely on everyone except DEV *and* GEORGE.

DEV

I watch. I watch him. Just like I always have. Like I have my entire
life. A face on a TV screen. I make small talk. I carry on with my
life. We carry on with our lives. Nothing changes. Everything, in
fact, stays exactly the same.

Lights shift.

13.

A photo of PERFORMER 4 *at the age of four is projected.*

PERFORMER 4
This is a picture of me at the age of [four]. As you can see, I was
doing my very best impression of being a little boy. Because I knew
that's what would make my mother happy. At this age right here, I
was obsessed with princesses. I used to have dreams that someone
would show up at my front door and unfurl this large scroll and
tell me, "You're actually next in line for the throne," and I'm like,
"Bitch, I'm outta here. Like, I am gone." In my head dreaming
they're gonna put me on a jet, like, they've been looking for me all
along! I grew up in the South, me and my grandparents and my
mom and brother lived in a two-bedroom apartment. For a time
me and my mom and brother shared a bed. Then my aunt stayed
with us for a time before she got pregnant. I didn't have my own
room until college. But I never saw us as poor. I was never hungry.
I know my mom made a lot of sacrifices so me and my brother
could have what we had.

The photo disappears.

I have always been fascinated with people who have more than me,
like, wow bitches really live like that! I don't think I've ever stopped
wanting to be a princess. But I wouldn't say I really gave a fuck
about the actual royal family until Meghan was involved—even
though, let's be honest that girl didn't even know she was Black
most of her life. But still, there's a soupçon of melanin there, so I
was like okay I'm paying attention. And now that she's gone, I'm

152

gone, I literally don't care again. It's like you think I gave a fuck about gymnastics before Gabby? Or tennis without Serena?

Anyway.

I went to college, I transitioned, moved to New York, and I got into ballroom and the kiki scene. They became my family. And one night we were voguing *down* on the pier, which people do over the summer, like, "Girl, let's pump to the pier, let's smoke a junz, let's grab a drink at the bar, and just go and ki." And it became this mini ball—

Sounds of the mini ball down on the pier.

PERFORMER 4 *begins to vogue.*

The scene eventually fades away and we return to the present of the theatre.

And when I won I got deemed Princess of the Pier by Quana, who's the Queen of the Kiki scene, no one's won more catego- ries, walked as many balls, she's the East Coast mother of Juicy Couture, which is my old house—she deemed me Princess of the Pier. This whole time you've been looking at a princess and you didn't even know it. When a group of marginalized people come together and deem each other royalty and give each other status it's never going to be rooted in how much they have. You're a legend or icon because you make it hot in your category. You're around. You know to run a house. You know how to be a mother, to give back, in the way you grace the stage, in the way you teach, in the way you love. It is earned. It is given and, girl, it can be taken away, so for now I am Princess of the Pier. And I know I'm not gaining anything other than respect and love from a community that has actually helped my life, in a way that the royals, that Meghan will never, my own government will never. Never. Like being on stage tonight with *(pointing)* [Performer 3], that means so much more to me than meeting the royals or the queen of England or whoever the fuck. I am honoured to be in your presence. To act alongside you. And to my grands Courtney, may I always speak your name. Someone once asked you on Instagram, "When should I transition?" And you replied with one word: today. That might not have been poetry to you, but that was poetry to me. *She* is opulence. *She* is royalty.

Who is a princess?
Who is a prince?
Who is a queen?
Who is divinely anointed? I ask you.
Who here is chosen by god?

 Silence.

I am.

 Pause.

I am chosen by god.
I am chosen by god.
And better.
I am chosen by those who love me.
This whole time you've been looking at a princess and you didn't even know it.

 Blackout.

 End of play.

On Prince Faggot
BY BRONTEZ PURNELL

Stated bluntly, Jordan Tannahill's *Prince Faggot* is a fairy tale. Refined, reflective, whip smart, and endearing, this play sets to tackle that flash moment in 2017 when a young Prince George visited a landing strip in Hamburg, Germany, looked at a helicopter in little boy wonder and adults of all ages took to the Internet to say, "Wow, he's visibly enjoying himself way too much—he's probably going to grow up to be a faggot . . ."

I was reading this and crying, 'cause, like, if I think about it, I (like many, perhaps) got called "faggot" well before I even knew what the goddamn word meant. For so long that I stopped being hurt and started responding, "That is correct, yes. How may I help you?"

At the core of the morality tale of this play is the moral conundrum of how very few of us (oh god, a prince even, or perhaps especially a prince?) are safe from the perils of unchecked (furthermore unwanted) perception.

Set in a hallucinogenic future (2032) and narrated in parts by a consciously correct chorus, the play deals in an alternate universe where Prince George DOES in fact grow up gay and finds his own Prince Charming—and the chaotic tumult and catharsis that erupts. Finding the love of one's life while the entire world is watching can in fact simultaneously be a fairy tale as well as a new form of hell; heaven help us all.

Now I can admit that I had my reservations about this play. Firstly, I am (I confess) a cultural swine piece of shit American who is so emotionally checked out on the subject of who exactly "the leaders of the free world" are that I approached this beautiful text with a headache.

Dear reader, I deeply implore you to understand that if I look across the linear timeline of what I recall of, like, my political engagement in life, all I can say I remember is partying WAY TOO MUCH during the Bush years (the second Bush years, to be exact) and having a very doubtful existence on paper during every other president I've lived through. And this is my experience IN MY OWN COUNTRY, MIND YOU—I don't think I've ever actually known a goddamn thing about the royal family of the United Kingdom. I shit you not when I tell you I actually had to google what their actual last name was because I had only ever referred to them as "the Royals" (apparently it's Windsor?).

The action of this play sets to spell out the endless conundrums of (included but not limited to) interracial sex, seemingly contradictory class positions amongst two loving homosexuals, dating a rich white boy, dating an Asian top, poppers, Communist Daddy issues, chaotic bottoms, "ew, my boyfriend is an art major, what will my parents think?" and also (somehow?) deep ruminations on contemporary dance. This is all tea.

Tannahill, in this offering, being both a concise and beautifully unjaded narrative, has done the heavy lifting of making these very celestial themes of love, duty, commitment, and—perhaps most importantly—abandon, and made them all earthbound.

At the brass tacks of the moral conundrum of all this drama is the simple fact that be one a divine normal or a future king, most people are (by laws of physics) widely incompatible.

How we deal with and move on from this problem is the stark definition of love.

Heaven help us all.

Brontez Purnell is the author of seven books, including 100 Boyfriends, *which won the* 2022 *Lambda Literary Award for Gay Fiction. The recipient of a* 2018 *Whiting Tennessee Williams Award for Fiction and the* 2022 *Foundation for Contemporary Arts Robert Rauschenberg Award for Risk Taking In Art, he was named one of the thirty-two Black Male Writers of Our Time by* T: The New York Times Style Magazine *in* 2018. *Purnell is also the front man for the band the Younger Lovers and a renowned performance artist and zine-maker.*

Staging Faggotry
BY HARI NEF

Faggotry, what and how a faggot does, precedes the faggot himself. Faggotry cries out inside of him, begging for release. "Let me out!" she shrieks, and inevitably he, the Faggot, must. If the Faggot's worth his salt, they'll put on a show together.

Prince Faggot is a show of Faggotry blazed to her hungriest, most dazzling ends. It shows us, in flesh, all of what Faggotry can be: plump scrota slapping in the throes of doggy-style, a grown man lisping under a bob wig, closed fists at the family table, shibari-shackled wrists, a femme queen voguing soft and cunt.

> A *photograph of Prince* GEORGE *of Wales, at the age of four, is projected.*

> **PERFORMER 1**: Prince George of Wales in 2017, gazing with limpid amazement at an ascending helicopter.

At top of show, Tannahill shows us the seed from which *Prince Faggot* sprung: a viral snap of a powerful, world-famous preschooler whose boyishness seems, in this moment, to have given way to girlish "amazement": knees buckled, wrists limpened, back arched. A boy's amazement is his disarmament, some fleeting submission to what he feels. But what of a boy's power? What happens when a particularly powerful boy, someday a powerful man, buckles his knees, limps his wrists, and arches his back? Is he collapsing? Abdicating?

For a prince, a single gesture can plunge an empire into anarchy, and a faggy gesture spells chaos. Faggotry coos, chants, and shrieks from within; she careens down a marble staircase in a nightgown underneath a chandelier. She seizes her host to ravish a nation, sever a family, or break a law.

It's not that Faggotry's out to catch a case (she doesn't even watch the news or pay her taxes!), it's that she burns within and *for* the faggot, whose body is for guiltless joy and whose heart is for boundless love—unless, of course, he asks to be bound! In that case, set the scene. And so does Tannahill: from high and low, with god and the devil, of paupers and princes.

Prince Faggot is a deliberate provocation. It's blue-chip clickbait, x-rated fanfic, and "punke" with an e—how Shakespeare spelled it to describe whores. *Prince Faggot* knows it's a massive fucking stunt because Jordan Tannahill is a massive fucking faggot—one of the best we've got, if you ask me. When Faggotry calls, Tannahill answers. He hoists her up, paints her fierce, tells her what to say, and walks her—leashed—on stage to lend us new ways of seeing, feeling, and hearing. Listen up: she's cooing, chanting, shrieking. Can or will you hear her? What does she want? Would it feel good? Does it scare you? Why? Why not?

Hari Nef is an actress and writer in New York City. Stage credits include The Seagull/Woodstock, NY *(The New Group),* Des Moines *(Theatre for a New Audience), and* "Daddy" *(The New Group, 2019), and she has appeared on screen in* Barbie, The Idol, You, Assasination Nation, *and* Transparent, *among many others. Nef's writing has been published in the* New York Times, Artforum, GQ, *and* Vice.

The Prince and The Faggot
BY DAVID VELASCO

I once dated a prince who wanted to be a faggot. He was cool and handsome, a vivid person. Also fucked like a racehorse. I'm a clay-coloured faggot who always thought of himself as royalty of some kind, even if it was severed from any origin. In this we weren't too unlike the characters in Jordan Tannahill's *Prince Faggot*, and because it's good art and an honest play about the power of projections, I imagine a lot of people might see themselves in it.

The prince and I seemed a good match, and we were in love. Maybe we still are. I introduced him to many faggots and women, and we had a lot of fun together. New York glamour fun. Parties that tumbled into the morning and sometimes the next afternoon and evening, powdered soups, holy sex. We also talked a lot, about real things. Read books, helped each other get to new places spiritually and intellectually. I don't think I've had conversations like that before or since. When my analyst friend talks about the phenomenon of "joining" I now have a strong feeling in my heart and head of what that means.

At some point things got too intense; we went down too many wrong paths. The idealizations soured and we realized that there were flaws behind our projections. This is normal in nearly any relationship, but sometimes it takes a stronger container to hold these kinds of epiphanies. You need to be able to stay in it long enough to get to the other side and see that some of the idealization is real and most of the projections are your own shit. The container we were in was cracked, for reasons too obscure to get into here.

If you believe in fairy tales like I do, you have to believe that people can continue to join after the projections fall away, that this is where a more serious joining comes in. You have to know that it's hard to do this alone or in a dyad, that it helps to have other people who can take on the splintered shards of fantasy that fly off as we burn through the idealization phase. You have to have a little faith that no one person is any one thing except when we all stand around them and make them so.

In the end, the prince felt like he wasn't allowed to be a faggot, and it was sad. To be honest, I think he embodied the real spirit of faggotry. But many of the ersatz faggots couldn't acknowledge their prince parts, their attachments to self-regard and shame around wealth and glamour, and things split. I say "in the end," but I also know that life isn't a fairy tale and that endings are as much an illusion as any projection. So, we shall see. Beginnings and endings are often twisty, just like they are in *Prince Faggot*, this beautiful story about all the obstacles we encounter as we try to patch ourselves together into our own imperfect, truthful prince-faggots.

David Velasco is a writer based in New York. He is currently at work on a memoir about the convergence of personal and political atrocity.

Acknowledgements

Like so much of what is beautiful and cherished in my life, I owe the existence of *Prince Faggot* to Jeremy O. Harris, who never stopped believing in it, and me.

I wrote the first draft of this play in the early days of the COVID-19 lockdown in London, and over the course of five years and three workshop processes, I fell in love, moved continents, and got married. Brandon Flynn, thank you for first sharing your talent, and then your life, with me.

I want to express my deep gratitude to . . .

Hari Nef, Brontez Purnell, and David Velasco for their reflections on *Prince Faggot,* and for allowing us to reprint their words alongside the play. These three essays were initially commissioned by Playwrights Horizons for *Almanac.*

To my co-conspirator Shayok Misha Chowdhury, to Jack Serio, Rachel Crowl, David Greenspan, K. Todd Freeman, Mihir Kumar, John McCrea, N'yomi Allure Stewart, Jason Veasey, Tyrone Mitchell Henderson, Sarah Lunnie, Montana Levi Blanco, Isabella Byrd, Lee Kinney, David Zinn, Ryan Gohsman, Zach Brecheen, Molly Pair, Cookie Jordan, UnkleDave's Fight-House, Deborah Hecht, and the entire creative team of the premiere production.

To Playwrights Horizons, in particular Adam Greenfield, Natasha Sinha, Casey York, Noah Silva, Lizzie Stern, Karl Baker Olson, Jay Janicki, Carol Almonte, Andrew Riedemann, Michael Graller, Matt Carlin, Jordan Best, Emily Zhou, Alaine Alldaffer, and Lisa Donadio.

ACKNOWLEDGEMENTS

To Soho Rep, in particular Caleb Hammons, Cynthia Flowers, Eric Ting, and Kaye Hurley.

To Studio Seaview, in particular Greg Nobile, Jonathan Whitton, Tony Marion, Anna Mack Pardee, Chase Parker, Jenna Ready, Austin Spero, Luca Fontes, Christophe Desorbay, and our understudies, Arewá Basit, Allen Gilmore, Rory Greenwood, and Keshav Moodliar.

To the catalyst of it all, bb², Jeremy O. Harris, Josh Godfrey, and Kayla Nicholson.

To Robert O'Hara and the actors who helped *Prince Faggot* along its journey, Alexandra Billings, Anand Desai-Barochia, Brandon Flynn, Francis Jue, Pooya Mohseni, Troye Sivan, Karan Soni, Stephen Spinella, as well as to Sue Wagner, John Johnson, Taylor Williams, Julian Sanchez, Jonny-James Kajoba, and Bryan Bauer.

To Salman Toor and Matthew Leifheit for generously allowing us to use their artwork.

To Alex Levy, Adam Eli, Blake Zidell, Caitlyn Tella, Jon Davies, Tony Kushner, Jason Weinberg, Phoebe Greenberg, Miles Greenberg, Thomas Rom, Andrew Tobias, Tricky Knot, Gabriel Araujo, James Dunne, and Alistair Wroe for their critical support.

To John MacGregor, Joe Machota, Imogen Sarre, Colin Rivers, Sue Carls, Angela Dallas, Sam Barickman, and Stephan Wetzel for taking such good care of me and my work.

As ever, to Annie Gibson, Blake Sproule, and Brandon Crone of Playwrights Canada Press.

And finally, to all the fetishists and freaks who supported and pushed me along the way.

Jordan Tannahill is a playwright, novelist, and director. His work has been translated into twelve languages and honoured with a number of prizes, including two Governor General's Literary Awards. His novel *The Listeners* was shortlisted for the 2021 Giller Prize and adapted into a limited series directed by Janicza Bravo for the BBC. In 2019, CBC Arts named Tannahill as one of sixty-nine LGBTQ Canadians, living or deceased, who have shaped the country's history.